Evidential Details

E-MAIL

I should certainly think that Titanic fans would eat this up, and revisit the testimony from the [Disaster] hearings, and see through the cover-up.

Yes I read the book. It was very compelling. I think that Mr. McMoneagle was right on. Together with the evidence you found from the formal hearings, the two fit together nicely. It answers questions that previously were filled with ambiguity. Things that just seemed odd, but could not quite be pinned down, in the original testimonies. Thanks for the great book. I feel satisfied it answers much of the mystery about Titanic's sinking.

Wow, verrrrrrrrrrrrry interesting stuff indeed. Someone is going to have to come up with a new Hollywood movie script and call it TITANIC - The Great Cover-up! [A] must read if you're a fan of RV and learning how it can be used to solve historical riddles and get down to the nitty gritty truth.

In general, it is a terrific story, and I think Joe has nailed two vital aspects, namely, the fact that...the lookouts [read book] ...and the other being the way Captain Smith's life ended.

Evidential Details

I find Joe's version to be in line with Smith's personality and with what an intellectually strong man would do. Apparently, nobody else has made such a conjecture. There is something about the...story that I find like the last piece of a jigsaw puzzle – it fits.

Yes, it made the case for further investigation into what happened to the Titanic and sheds more light on new leads and research for historians.

Just finished reading Titanic and again loved it. Found it fascinating the remote viewing after the last boat left and (the) Captain opened the (find out). How very sad to know your fate. The description of the Captain and the remaining passengers in the first class drawing room after the last boat left was amazing. Felt as if I was watching from above, the detail was very clear. Thanks for the brilliant reads.

I read with care the latest Titanic volume, and find it really fascinating.... This is such a fascinating story! I am still wondering how to get you into the big leagues, with wide spread attention, as I think your series deserves.

Evidential Details

Medals Received

Legion of Merit   Meritorious Service

Citations

Meritorious Service with **one** Oak Leaf Cluster;[1]
Army Commendation with **two** Oak Leaf Clusters, Presidential Unit;
Meritorious Unit with **three** Oak Leaf Clusters;
Vietnam Gallantry Cross with Palm for gathering enemy intelligence for Allied counter offensives.

---

[1] The same medal cannot be given twice. When exemplary service is again rendered, the Oak Leaf Cluster (OLC) is attached in place of a second identical medal.

Evidential Details

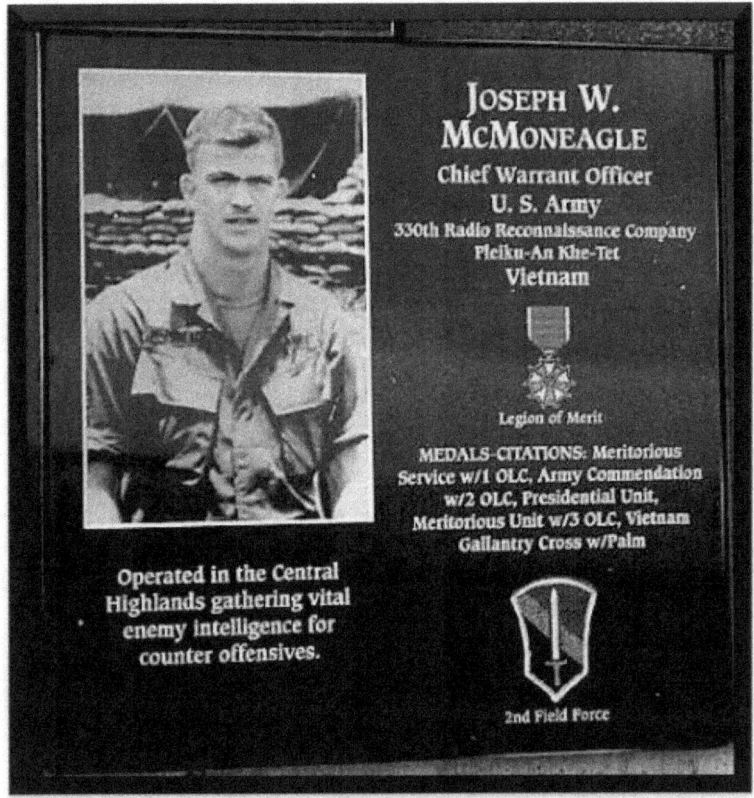

The Bronze Plaque on the Veterans Memorial Wall

In what is clearly the most fascinating component of U.S. Military History, Joseph McMoneagle is the only man in world history to be awarded a medal for consistent accuracy in Remote Viewing (Psy-functioning) by a military. As *Operation Star Gate's* Number 1 Military Intelligence asset at Fort Meade, Maryland, he was the Pentagon's go to man when secret data could not be obtained by any other means or was time sensitive.

Evidential Details

The Quick Take

(The) authority to award the Legion of Merit Medal is reserved for general officers and flag officers in pay grade O-9 (e.g., [for] Lieutenant General and Vice Admiral) and above... - Wikipedia.

At least two witnesses must submit seven forms for proper medal determination. Based on the quality of the information, Military Decorations personnel selected the medal with the following language.

*The award is given for service rendered in a clearly exceptional manner. For service not related to actual war the term **"key individual"** applies to a narrower range of positions than in time of war and requires **evidence of significant achievement**. In peacetime, service should be in the nature of a special requirement or of an **extremely difficult duty** performed in an unprecedented and **clearly exceptional manner**.*

Unites States Legion of Merit Medal bestowal requirements.

Once it was demonstrated what this soldier could do, these Services used his services:

During his career, Mr. McMoneagle has provided...informational support to the Central Intelligence Agency **(CIA)**, *Defense Intelligence Agency* **(DIA)**, *National Security Agency* **(NSA)**, *Drug Enforcement Agency* **(DEA)**, *Secret Service, Federal Bureau of Investigation* **(FBI)**, *United States Customs* **(ICE)**, *the National Security Council* **(NSC)**, *most major commands* **(Army, Navy, Air Force, Intelligence)** *within the Department of Defense* **(DOD)**, *and hundreds of other individuals, companies, and corporations.*

Paragraph from Mr. McMoneagle's CV.

Evidential Details

The Evidential Details Mystery Series

Decorated United States Military Intelligence Psychic Remote Viewer solves some of History's Greatest Mysteries

TITANIC

AFTER THE LAST LIFEBOAT

SEEDS/MCMONEAGLE

2011

THE LOGISTICS NEWS NETWORK, LLC.

Evidential Details

Published on the Evidential Details
Imprint, a Division of
Logistics News Network, LLC
Inbox@LNN1.com

RV Session Work © 1997 All rights reserved
Updated Edition Copyright 2011 by S.J. Seeds

The Evidential Details Mysteries Series
Titanic – After the Last Lifeboat includes biographical references.
ISBN: 978-0-9826928-2-0

Steamship Lines – Twentieth Century Sea Disasters – United States Maritime History – U.S. Senate Hearings, 1912 – White Star Line – British Maritime History – British Disaster Hearings, 1912 – Titanic - J. Bruce Ismay – Captain E.J. Smith - McMoneagle, Joseph – Puthoff, PhD., Dr. Harold E. – Remote Viewing – Stanford Research Institute – Neurophysiology - Anomalous Cognition - Quantum Mechanics

Library of Congress Card Number: 2010904635

Book design by LNN.
Printed in the United States of America

If you are unable to purchase this, or our other history books in your local bookstore, visit our web site at www.LNN1.com

All rights reserved. No part of this book may be reproduced or transmitted in any form or by means, electronic or mechanical, including photocopying or by any information storage and retrieval system without the written permission of the Publisher under International and Pan American Copyright Conventions.

Evidential Details

Table of Contents

The Quick Take..6

Acknowledgment...10

Preface 11

Introduction: The former Princess Diana Spencer's auto accident..........13

Part II

Target - R.M.S. Titanic

Chapter One – The Lookout's Secret......................................45

Chapter Two – The Captain's Unknown Death......................93

Bibliography...140

Part III

Credentials..142

Human Use..144

A Chinese Encounter...145

The Military's Remote Viewing Protocols..............................147

Beginnings: The CIA's Stanford University remote viewing program......152

Targeted Reading..172

Additional Taskings...175

Evidential Details

Acknowledgement

The author would like to gratefully acknowledge the hours spent by Joseph McMoneagle. He is a peerless individual and will be understood for generations as an exceptional scientific pioneer into the human brain and the probable co-incarnational condition of our three dimensional existence. I want to thank all the others in the original unit that I have met, or corresponded with, or telephoned, or studied under, or simply shook hands with.

I would like to acknowledge the people of the Monroe Institute™ whose pioneering programs do so much to help people understand the possibilities of the human mind. And to Lyn Buchanan's military-like classroom that may be the last place for the public to get instruction in this format.

I want to thank Craig for his patience, support and feedback. And also to the volunteer editors who gave of their time to edit the first six volumes just for the opportunity to be the world's first to read the series through.

And then to all the positive and truly fascinated people who grasped the concept. It was these, of every persuasion, whose judgment it was that this information be brought forward.

Evidential Details

Preface

Many agree these books can affect history - for two reasons: findings and methodologies. For the first time, Military Intelligence quality Controlled Remote Viewing capabilities have been brought to solve historical mysteries in what academia refers to as *recent modern* – the exception being the Ötzi The Iceman material, which was designed to support scientific inquiry at the Museum in Bolzano, Italy. This effort was to develop the most accurate historical information possible. Time will tell as individuals, with peripheral research, provide anecdotal information or produce a document that suddenly fits.

Others have gone so far as to say these findings unlock more new data than any particular PhD candidate's History dissertation this year. And it is for this prospect that the reader is encouraged to look deeper into the ulterior motives for opposition. For an indication as to the difficulties bringing this manuscript forward, the reader is referred to Jim Marr's Foreword in Lyn Buchanan's book *The Seventh Sense* [Paraview, ©2003] For information about the origins of the military's involvement with Remote Viewing, kindly refer to Beginnings. The Princess Diana Spencer Introduction was designed to answer questions about nomenclature, viewer integrity and data quality.

For any researcher, it is the guarded realization that you have connected unattainable investigational dots that is the most intellectually stimulating factor in any horizon field of inquiry. My decade of documenting those points seem to confirm the viability of Remote Viewing as a research tool when used in conjunction with other research sources. What I can say is that I have been involved with the most spectacularly fascinating process of historical inquiry ever. As likely the only author to begin historical research with solutions in hand, I came to call these new confirmational dots the *Evidential Details*.

Evidential Details

Military Targeting Follow-up

"Det G's [1] viewers looked at projects ranging from the status of a cement plant in a hostile country to the location of Soviet troops in Cuba. Important North Korean personalities were targeted, as well as underground facilities in Europe, chemical weapons in Afghanistan, the presence of electronic bugs in the new U.S. embassy in Moscow, the activities of a KGB general officer, a missing U.S. helicopter, tunnels under the Korean Demilitarized Zone, and numerous buildings whose purposes were unknown to U.S. intelligence."

"But frequently we never learned how close we had come to the truth, how helpful we had been, or even what we had been looking for in the first place. The targets were sometimes so highly classified that substantive evaluations could not be provided."[i]

[i] Smith, Paul H., *Reading the Enemy's Mind – Inside Star Gate, America's Psychic Espionage Program*; Tor Non-fiction, 2005

Military Remote Viewing vs. Store Front Psychics

"In actual practice, the psychic produces these disconnected phrases and hopes that one of them will trigger something in the customer's unconscious mind, providing the "psychic" answer. Random utterances not having a definite meaning can always be twisted and reshaped to mean virtually anything that fits the situation. There are many "psychics" who have taken this type of gibberish to a finely honed skill."

Lyn Buchanan – *The Seventh Sense*

---

[1] Det G [Detachment G] was the remote viewing program's code name as it evolved from Operation 'Gondola Wish' to Operation 'Grill Flame'. These were the viewers to make the Army's cut between December 1978 and January 1979. "The Army Chief of Staff for Intelligence, Major General Thompson, officially decreed that the program name, embodied in Det G, would be the focal point for all Army involvement in parapsychology and remote viewing." Op cit. Smith

Introduction

An
Introduction
To Remote Viewing

A review of the terminology, history and capabilities targeting

The Former Princess Of Wales Diana Spencer's 1997 Auto Accident

(For the cover story, please refer to the Table of Contents)

> "*When they* (University researchers) *did produce an incredibly accurate response during an experiment, it was in even a moderate sense "unnerving." In a greater sense, it was "earth shattering." As* (Stanford PhD) *Russell* (Targ) *implied, for some it was even "terrifying." In no case, was it ever taken lightly, as it always had a tendency to alter one's perspective towards reality and/or our place within it.*"
> ~ Medal Recipient Joseph W. McMoneagle~

Princess Diana Introduction

It was the peak of the Twentieth Century's Cold War [1945-1990]. The United States, the old Soviet Union, and the People's Republic of China were striving to find new ways to get an intelligence edge. During the years 1968 to 1972, the United States obtained reports that scientists in the Soviet Union had had some success with a telekinesis program that introduced atrial fibulation into frog hearts causing a heart attack. Realizing the program could target key military and political leaders, and so driven by a threat assessment, the Central Intelligence Agency funded a Stanford University think tank in Menlo Park, California - the Stanford Research Institute (SRI) - to conduct an analysis about what humanity through the ages has pondered.

The doctors were to determine scientifically if psy-functioning could be taught, quantified and directed within written protocols. If so, did this represent a credible threat to the people of the United States? Their highly classified "Black Ops" program lasted from early 1972 until November 1995.

Under the most extensive and stringent experimentation that two PhD's could devise, the SRI, supported by other labs and the Army, developed mankind's first "psychic" protocols. "This led to greater understanding of everything from methods of evaluation, to establishing statistical standards, to how a human brain might be appropriately studied."[i] When their findings were made public, many in the academic community were privately stunned.

Eventually this covert military effort focused on real world data collection. As the years of research, analysis and application moved through the 1970's and 80's, Army brass with wholly personal motives, would attempt to quash the program even when research costs did not impact their budget. "All the funding had been approved on a year-to-year basis, and only then based on how effective the unit was in supporting the tasking agencies. These reviews were made semi-annually at the Senate and House select subcommittee level, where the work results were reviewed within the context in which it was happening."[ii]

Fortunately, for The People, the program was given different code names and moved around various Defense budgets until much of the research and development was completed. What emerged was an incredibly "robust" database - and a process -

Introduction

referred to as Controlled Remote Viewing [CRV].[1]

Much of the work took place within the 902nd United States Army Intelligence Group at Fort Meade, Maryland, whose barracks have been demolished. However, from the fastidiously maintained database emerged statistically advanced practitioners; world class viewers whose RV data was the "best in the business." Among these, one remote viewer was the first in history to be decorated with the Army's Legion of Merit and Meritorious Service Awards (with five Oak Leaf Clusters) for having made key contributions to the Intelligence community. This same individual was tasked to unlock the mysteries in this Evidential Details Book Series.

Obviously, accuracy is the name of the game. As with any horizon application process purposefully moving the human brain into the sub-quark level of quantum mechanics required new clinical terminology. As the CRV process was tested, protocols written and cautiously modified, scientists documented mental hazards to viewer accuracy. These hindrances were cataloged and their characteristics differentiated. Year after year laboratory research determined accurate mental representations could be inhibited in a variety of ways. Some of these mental distracters included:

Physical Inclemency - Knowledge of an expected disruption like a phone call or someone about to arrive during a remote viewing session.

Advanced Visuals - A fleeting thought you cannot get rid of before a session.

Emotional Distracters or Attractors - An image you do or do not want to view regardless of the tasking.

Front Loading - Knowledge of what the target is before the viewing session. If localized, it can be used in targeting a feature within the whole picture, perhaps a house in a meadow in front of a mountain. However, without neutral wording like "The target is man-made" the object is generally rendered unworkable.

Analytic Overlay [AOL] - If a viewer is not informed about the target and not front loaded but still has personal information about it, that

---

[1] This may also stand for Coordinate Remote Viewing when longitudinal and latitudinal target coordinates are used.

Princess Diana Introduction

knowledge may pollute the information stream rendering the session unworkable. Analytic Overlay can be a problem for any viewer. According to the military's former #1 remote viewer:

Joseph McMoneagle - Analytic overlay - CRV [Controlled Remote Viewing], **as a format or method for learning remote viewing, offers a structure within which you can discard or identify specific elements within a session for which you are certain or not certain. Analytic Over-Lay (AOL) being a common label for something that falls within the "uncertain" category. However, when studied (under laboratory conditions), there is evidence that fifty percent of the time, information labeled as AOL actuality, wasn't.**

I have observed just as many times, someone being smacked up against the side of the head while attempting CRV because they had strayed from the given format and slipped into AOL. I think that sometimes you may forget that CRV was developed within the hallowed halls of SRI and was taught there for years. I saw very little difference in the AOL pitfalls with CRV and other methodologies. I did see that to some extent it was a highly polished technique, which was more easily transferred through training.

With this quick overview of the subconscious transference of recollections, we turn to the remote viewing of the Princess Diana Spencer's accident in the early morning hours of August 31, 1997. As this researcher found, how one targets is critical to the result. In the fall of 1997, the massive press coverage of Princess Diana's accident and funeral emerged as a very real overlay problem. The Hotel Ritz in Paris, France rather than the crash site was targeted. There had been much less news coverage at the hotel. At the time, this target was less than two months old. No accident report had been completed. An envelope, with a second target envelope inside, had been mailed to Joseph McMoneagle's home with nothing more than the targeting coordinates and a date. A skeptical *Life Magazine* reporter was on hand as an observer to write a story.

Mr. McMoneagle requested I submit a target. The viewing event started at 11:49 am on October 29, 1997. What makes these sessions interesting is that the reader can sense the Intelligence intellect. Having viewed 1200 targets in just the last two years of the

Introduction

military's Operation Star Gate alone, this job would reasonably have been assigned to the only viewer to participate in the program for twenty-three years. What was submitted was:
Target Envelope No. 102997 - (no additional information other than what's sealed within the envelope.)

* * *

As her size nine shoes hit the airport tarmac the former Princess of Wales Diana Spencer, 36, knew she was entitled to an escort by that special branch of the French Interior Ministry charged with guarding visiting dignitaries - the Service de Protection des Hautes Personalities (SPHP). But there would be no need of the service once she left the airport. This was to be a private visit.

Diana was returning from a yachting vacation in the Mediterranean off Northeast Sardinia. She and Emad "Dodi" Al-Fayed, [1955-1997] had been aboard the Fayed family's $27 million dollar (US$39.5m/2015), 195 foot yacht *Jonikal*, with 16 crew members.

At this point, "...in her relationship with Dodi Fayed she was displaying a new facet. In some ways a late developer, she had grown up and was simply having some adult fun."[iii] But the couple had been stalked by high-speed paparazzi boats wherever they went. On their last afternoon, they came ashore at the Cala de Volpe in Sardinia and the, "Paparazzi swarmed around them like bees, flashing away."[iv] Forced back to the boat, "Things came to a head when a scuffle broke out between three paparazzi and several members of the *Jonikal*'s crew."[v]

At about the same time, hundreds of miles away, a 73 year-old grandfather, Edward Williams, walked into the police station in Mountain Ash, Mid Glamorgan, Wales. He reported to the police he had had a premonition Princess Diana was going to die. The police log, time stamped 14:12 hours on August 27, 1997, stated:

"He [Williams] *said he was a psychic and predicted that Princess Diana was going to die. In previous years he has predicted that the Pope and Ronald Reagan were going to be the victims of assassination. On both occasions he was proven to be correct. Mr. Williams*

Princess Diana Introduction

appeared to be quite normal."[vi]

Based on his previous record the police passed this report along to the department's Special Branch Investigative Unit.

Fed up with the non-stop press hassle, on Saturday August 30, Dodi and Diana boarded the Fayed's Gulfstream IV jet at Olbia airport in Sardinia and flew north. They arrived at Le Bourget Airport about 10 miles north of Paris, France at 3:20 p.m. Fayed's butler Rene Delorm recalled, "Unfortunately, we had a welcoming committee of about ten paparazzi waiting for us."[vii] About 600 feet (183 meters) away was a Mercedes and a Range Rover. "We had all seen the paparazzi, so we moved quickly. We wanted to get out of the plane and into the cars as fast as possible. (Body Guard) Trevor (Rees-Jones) was the first out of the jet..."[viii]

The entourage had a police escort from the airport up to France's highway A-1 leading to Paris. But as they entered the expressway, reporter's cars and two man motorcycle teams immediately dogged them. The paparazzi were armed with powerful, maximum strength, flashes to penetrate deep into the car. Philippe Dourneau, 35, was Dodi's chauffeur. But in the Range Rover vehicle there had been a switch. Assistant Chief of Hotel Security Henri Paul was at the wheel. It is unclear why Paul was chauffeuring and not at the Ritz Hotel as acting Security Chief.

Once on the highway, Dodi instructed Dourneau to pick up speed in an attempt to elude photographers. What ensued was a high-speed pursuit with motorcycle cameramen weaving in and out shooting pictures. The motorcycle whirl was so intense Diana reportedly cried out in alarm that someone could get killed.[ix]

"Then a black car sped ahead of us and ducked in front of the Mercedes, braking and making us slow down so the paparazzi on motorcycles could get more pictures. They were risking their lives and ours, just to get a shot of Dodi and Diana riding in a car. "*Unbelievable*", exclaimed butler Rene Delorm.[x]

Dodi was not accustomed to this and after their high seas harassment, his patience was running thin. Pursuing for miles, the paparazzi then used phones to notify photographers ahead to form another gauntlet on the next highway segment. The Fayed cars split

Introduction

up in an attempt to divide the photographers. Some pursued Henri Paul as he drove to Dodi's apartment to deliver the luggage.

Finally, the Mercedes made it to Bois de Boulogne on the outskirts of Paris to visit the Fayed's Windsor Villa. They arrived about 3:45 p.m. Then they were off to the Ritz Hotel in downtown Paris at 4:35. Alerted by the cameramen the hotel entrance was packed with photographers which in turn generated curiosity seekers in the general public.

Once inside the hotel, Diana checked into the second floor Imperial Suite and went to have her hair done. She also made some phone calls. After the accident, London's *Daily Mail* correspondent Richard Kay stated that Diana had called him saying she was going to complete her contractual obligations through November and then go into private life.

Another call was made to psychic Rita Rogers whom Diana had been in contact with since 1994. Just three weeks earlier, on August 12, Dodi and Di had visited Rogers for a reading on Dodi. She warned him not to go driving in Paris. "*I saw a tunnel, motorcycles, there was this tremendous sense of speed.*"[xi] Uneasy, Rogers reminded Diana about her readout concerning a Parisian tunnel saying, "*...remember what I told Dodi.*"[xii]

At seven o'clock, they left the hotel for Dodi's apartment at Rue 1 Arsene-Houssaye arriving at 7:15 p.m. Here the couple found the street so crowded they could not even open the car door. "The paparazzi literally mobbed the couple," said (32 year old former Royal Marine Kes) Wingfield. "They really disturbed and frightened the Princess, even though she was used to this. These paparazzi were shouting, which made them even more frightening. I had to push them back physically.'"[xiii]

From their third floor apartment, butler Rene recalled:

"*...I could see they were being mobbed. I heard the shouting, saw the flashes going off and watched a security guard shove one of the photographers. Dodi did his best to shield Diana as Trevor and Kes fought to clear a path to the door...The princess was ashen and trembling, and Dodi was angry as they stalked through the apartment door...*"[xiv]

This was the way it was going to be. Rumors were rife about

Princess Diana Introduction

a marriage proposal and some wealthy publishers made it clear big money was available to the photographer that got the "million dollar shot". But no million dollars had been budgeted.

Later, after things settled down and Dodi had returned from shopping for two rings at the Repossi Jewelry Boutique, Rene recounted, "I met Dodi as he walked through the kitchen doorway, his eyes gleaming with excitement. It was then that he showed me the ring.[2] *'Make sure we have champagne on ice when we come back from dinner,'* he told me urgently. *'I'm going to propose to her tonight!'*"[xv] Elated, he also phoned this proposal news to his cousin Hassan Yassin that evening.[xvi]

Dodi had the Hotel staff book a 9:45 p.m. dinner reservation at the fashionable restaurant Chez Benoit on the Rue Saint Martin. He also phoned the Ritz staff he would not be returning. As a result, Security Chief Henri Paul departed for the weekend at 7:05 p.m.

At 9:30 p.m., Dodi and Diana left the apartment for dinner but could not get through the crowd at the restaurant entrance. It was clear they could not enter a restaurant together. The enormous number of paparazzi forced Dodi to cancel their night out. The Press was controlling his special night with his special lady. A frustrated Dodi decided they should make the four mile drive to the Hotel Ritz where they could dine in France's only "safe" restaurant. But Security Chief Henri Paul had gone for the week-end and the abrupt change left the hotel staff with no time to prepare for their arrival.

When they arrived at the Ritz, another press riot broke out. It took Diana two whole minutes to negotiate the camera gauntlet the 20 feet from the front door drive-up to the hotel turnstile. The security camera time stamped her entrance at 9:53 p.m. Security man Wingfield said:

"*I had to protect her physically from the paparazzi, who were coming really too close to her*[.] *Their cameras were right next to her face.*"[xvii]

Dodi was furious and started shouting at his employ-ees about no security to shield the 10-second walk up from the driveway. Shaken, the press savvy Diana wept in the lobby. Every-one was

---

[2] Dodi received a US$100,000/month ($146.500/2015) allowance from his father.

Introduction

upset. With the owner's son angry, and the security force completely embattled, a decision was made to call the Security Chief back to work. Francois Tendil called Henri Paul's cell phone at 9:55 p.m. Once safely in their room, Dodi called his father Mohammed Al-Fayed at approximately 10:00 p.m. He said the two would announce their engagement the next week when Diana returned from England.[xviii] "Diana always had the children for the last few days before they went back to school at the start of a new term, so that she could get everything ready and make sure they had the right kit."[xix] On Friday, she had called to confirm her boys would be at the airport to meet her on Sunday morning.

Dinner was ordered from the hotel's Imperial Suite restaurant. Diana's last meal was scrambled eggs with mushrooms and asparagus, then vegetable tempura with fillet of sole. As Di and Dodi were trying to dine normally, Henri Paul pushed his way back into the hotel through the paparazzi.

For this targeting, the Hotel Ritz Building was tasked using the proper date, time, and location coordinates. As Mr. McMoneagle looked at a double blind envelope, he started:

McMoneagle - I find myself standing next to a man who is inside some kind of a public building. He is approximately five feet, ten inches in height, good build, good condition physically. He weighs about 165 pounds, is clean shaven, light brown hair, right handed, 38-40 years of age, and is not British or American; meaning he probably has another language other than English as his native tongue.[3]

Upon his return, Henri Paul waited around the Ritz for about two hours. He allegedly had a couple drinks at the bar. The Ritz security cameras recorded his behavior which would be used for future analysis. As Chief of Security, he was certainly aware of their placement and recording capabilities.

McMoneagle - Building interior - Where he (Paul) is within the building is inside of a very elaborate corridor. It runs the full length of the building and has lots of gilded paint, mirrors, thick carpets, lots of flowers, and is very fancy. The

---

[3] Paul was 167 lbs. and he was 41 years old. He had brown hair and was also balding. His native language was French. He spoke fluent English and some German.

Princess Diana Introduction

Session Sketch

This drawing provides a rare glimpse intelligence level RV artwork. In this exercise, people and not the building were targeted. But, this sketch could be the third floor at the North Korean Embassy in Moscow, Russia, or any building, anywhere, anytime. As a person was the target, the Hotel Ritz Paris first floor was roughed out at midnight on August 31, 1997. Points of interest are:

1) At the top of the page, the words **Big Bldg** appear;
2) The various circles with an **X** inside indicates where people were standing at approximately 12:15 a.m. on August 31, 1997.
3) On the left, the **Main Door** is shown with an **X** representing the doorman. As the hall extends to the right, the various rooms are notated.
4) Toward the bottom is a **Business** area. As you walk from the front door, **"There is an area off to the right of this corridor which has a lot of dark paneling and dark colors with a long bar or type of counter."**
5) At the top is an **Alcove** with two people inside. These individual's backgrounds – conversations – futures – mental states - deaths can be targeted at any time in the future.
6) Where the hallway comes to a junction there is a **Man**. This is Henri Paul as he monitors the activities in both corridors. What were Paul's private thoughts? **"I associate him with a car which is parked outside and he is thinking about this car, or it seems to occupy his thoughts for some reason."**
7) Behind Henri Paul is the **Laborer Area**. Next to this is the drawing date and time documenting who was where when.
8) The hallway to the **Side Door**, **"...intersects with some kind of a smaller staff or receiving area; perhaps a back door to the building. It is recessed and that is where his car is parked."** That recessed area is shown.
9) McMoneagle also shows the **Formal Black Limo**'s position by the back door and correctly identified the automobile's color and manufacturer's hood ornament (bottom right).

Introduction

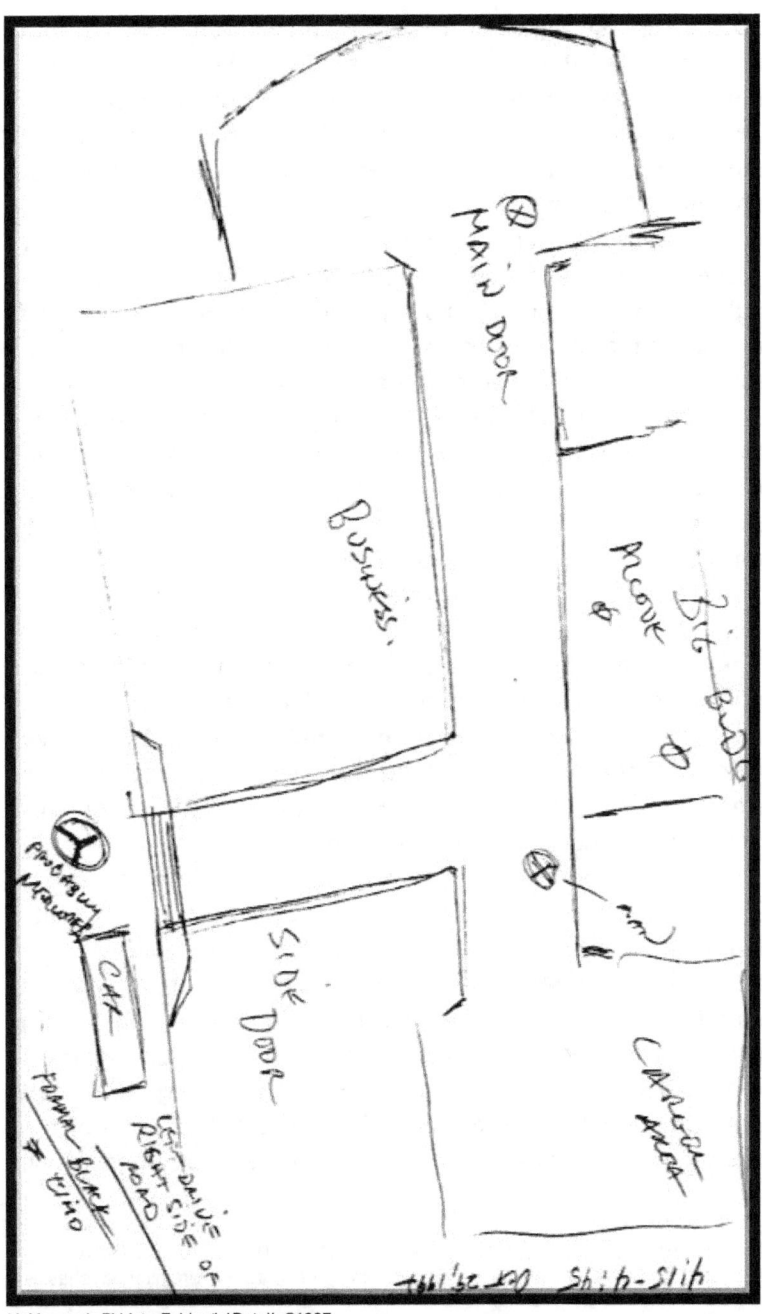

McMoneagle RV Art – Evidential Details ©1997
Hotel Ritz Paris first floor with Mercedes (lower right) as viewed from Virginia.

Princess Diana Introduction

corridor runs straight out to a front entry which is well lit and very busy (even though my sense is that it is very late at night). There is an area off to the right of this corridor which has a lot of dark paneling and dark colors with a long bar or type of counter. So, this may be the reception area of the hotel or something like that.

Where he (Paul) **is standing is where the main corridor intersects with a short corridor that runs off at a ninety degree angle to the left. It intersects with some kind of a smaller staff or receiving area; perhaps a back door to the building. It is recessed and that is where his car is parked.**

The Etoile Limousine Company manager Jean-Francis Musa, 39, provided six luxury cars to the Ritz Hotel for their exclusive use. This Mercedes was licensed as a Grande Remise auto meaning only a licensed chauffeur was authorized to drive it. Henri Paul did not possess those credentials.

McMoneagle - Driver orientation - I believe that he (Paul) **drives a cab or limo...on the side, because I associate him with a car, which is parked outside and he is thinking about this car, or it seems to occupy his thoughts for some reason. He is mostly interested with driving from point A to point B. I believe he is not alone and get a strong feeling of mixed male/female in energy; which either means his passenger will be gay, or consist of two people--a male and a female.**

Limo is not a stretch limo but a short, black and formal kind of car. I get an impression of a Mercedes emblem or some kind of emblem like that, so I'm assuming it is a very expensive car, could be a Mercedes.[4] **It is formal and black with an extended foot space in the back seat. Four doors. It is very heavy and my sense is that it might be equipped for important passengers** — e.g., **bullet proof glass, armoring, hardened tires, etc.; which leads me to believe that at least one of the passengers** [Trevor Rees-Jones, 29] **might be a body-guard** [but]

---

[4] The Mercedes S 280 sedan, valued at about $100,000 (US$159.292/2018) was engineered with eight advanced safety systems. The car had a reinforced chassis and roof. It had energy absorbing front and rear end crumple zones with electronic traction control. It also had an electronic ESP sensing system, which monitored trajectory with wheel speed to sense cornering speeds.

Introduction

this may be Analytic overlay caused by the excessive feelings of security surrounding this vehicle and driver.

* * *

Information about Henri Paul's mixed motivations have come to light in the years since the accident. Born one of five brothers on July 3, 1956 in the port town of Lorient, France, he had a Bachelors Degree in Mathematics and Science from the Lycee St. Louis and had won several contests for his skill as a classical pianist. He became a pilot in 1976 but was unable to qualify as a jet fighter pilot when he joined the French Air Force in 1979. Paul did however achieve the rank of Lieutenant while assigned to Security in the French Air Force Reserves.

In 1986, Paul helped setup Ritz Security. He went on to become Assistant Director. On the day of the accident, he was carrying 12,560 francs (US $2,280) and his savings account passbook.[5] Where the money came from is unknown, but he was one of only two men in France that had access to the automobile conversations of Dodi and Di. The ability to advise the press of their plans would have been of great value.

Personal adversity. Henry Paul had recently been passed over for promotion a second time by Hotel Ritz management. The first disappointment had come on Jan 1, 1993 when the nod went to colleague Jean Hocquet even though Paul was obviously in position as the number two security man. Now again, effective June 30, 1997, as "Deputy Chief" he became the defacto head of a twenty person security team while Ritz Management searched for another chief. Now vulnerable, Paul had been informed of this exactly one month before the accident.

Post mortem tests stated Paul had consumed two antidepressants called Fluoxetine and Tiapride before the accident. Fluoxetine is the active ingredient in Prozac and together these drugs are commonly used to fight alcoholism. When alcohol is

---

[5] Henri Paul may have charged the equivalent of US$2,250 (1997) per surveillance event and simply had an additional $30 pocket money that day. His salary was reported at $40,000 ($63,716/2018) per year.

introduced, the intoxicant effect is multiplied. On September 17, a more sophisticated laboratory's final report was issued. It stated that Henri Paul had been in, "*moderate chronic alcoholism for a minimum of one week.*"[xx] Once this became public, the Ritz's attorneys and Mohammed Al-Fayed found themselves on the defensive. An unlicensed employee now appeared criminally negligent in a multiple wrongful death accident while in Hotel Ritz employment. It became the million dollar shot vs. the Al-Fayeds.

The intoxication driving limit in France is 0.50 grams per liter. One lab report stated Henri Paul's blood alcohol level was 1.87 g/l. This is the equivalent drinking time for eight or nine shots of whiskey in what was found to be an empty stomach. A second, private laboratory's more moderate findings were used in the Final Report. The Paris Prosecutor's Office Report stated:

"*On this particular point, numerous expert's reports examined following the autopsy on the body of Henri Paul rapidly showed the presence of a level of pure alcohol per litre of blood of between 1.73 and 1.75 grams, which is far superior, in all cases, than the legal level.*
 Similarly, these analyses revealed as [did] *those carried out on samples of the hair and bone marrow of the deceased, that he regularly consumed Prozac and Tiapridal, both medicines which are not recommended for drivers, as they provoke a change in the ability to be vigilant, particularly when they are taken in combination with alcohol.*"[xxi]

So had Henri Paul been out drinking? It is known he returned to the Ritz two hours and fifty minutes after departing. But no one knew where he was when he received the Ritz phone call. Investigations into who had seen Paul failed to provide a single witness. In Paris, in the fall of 1997, there was a real fear of liability for anyone acknowledging Paul had been drinking in their establishment. Nonetheless, the French media reported "*someone*" saw Paul drinking "aperitifs" between 7:05 and 10:08 p.m. that evening. "Someone" is wide open. It means that after he got the call to return at 9:55 p.m., he dallied almost another quarter-hour before departing which is hard to believe given everyone's concerns. Until now, the critical question about where and what Paul was doing before returning to the hotel remains unknown.

Introduction

McMoneagle - I think he was in fact sitting in a small restaurant or coffee shop, very near where he lives. Maybe even on the corner near his house. He was alone as far as I can tell. I think he was in fact drinking coffee. I do not think he was depressed, at least not more than usual. Also, regardless of what might be said, I DID NOT get a sense that he was drunk. It is remotely possible that he was taking some kind of a medication but I doubt it.

Coffee! Not drunk! This flew in the face of the formal investigation. We were now privately aware, months before the controversy started, Henri Paul was not drunk.

Henri Paul was a pilot. Research indicated it was impossible to reconcile allegations of alcoholism with Paul's recent physical examination. Unbeknownst to the authorities issuing the report, just two days before the accident, Paul had completed a "rigorous" physical examination to renew his pilot's license. His *Certificat D'Aptitude Physique et Mentale* showed, "No signs of alcoholism."[xxii] A direct medical conflict supporting McMoneagle. Was Paul really fighting alcoholism? Six months after these ses-sions, the Ritz Hotel security videos further reaffirmed our data.

Behavioral Psychologist Dr. Martin Skinner commented in Fulcrum Productions documentary for ITV. The doctor stated there were no behavioral signs of drunkenness as Henri Paul waited for Dodi and Diana.

Skinner: *I don't think there is evidence, from the video, that can suggest he looked drunk. The pictures of him walking up and down the corridor are straight and smooth. He is standing very still and there is nothing in his demeanor, from these videos, to suggest that there are any problems with his competence in this situation.*[xxiii]

Next came a statement from Trevor Rees-Jones, the front seat bodyguard sitting next to Paul. About intoxication, he said:

Rees-Jones: *I had no reason to suspect he was drunk. He did not look or sound like he had been drinking. He just seemed his normal self. He was working. He was competent. End of story. I can state quite categorically that he was not a hopeless drunk as some have tried to suggest. I like to think I have enough intelligence to see if the guy was plastered or not – and he wasn't.*[xxiv]

Princess Diana Introduction

Neither the bodyguards, nor Dodi, or anyone else at the Hotel detected anything unusual in Paul's behavior. But there was more.

Paul's blood was next reported as containing abnormally high carbon monoxide levels - twenty percent too much. How this happened has never been determined. But doctors agree it is impossible for a forty year old man, with that much poison in his blood stream, not to look and feel sick - too sick for high speed urban driving. When the press advanced the idea car exhaust was the source of Paul's poisoning, Dodi's father, Mohammed Al-Fayed, put the obvious question: *"How did Henri Paul get 20% carbon monoxide in his blood when my son had none?"*[xxv]

The obvious question is how you can get that much CO^2 into someone's blood stream when, due to an instantaneous death there was no breathing, and the engine had stopped.

During his last month Henri Paul had come to know what it was like to assume the Security Chief's responsibilities while the Ritz Hotel interviewed. He must have been concerned an outside hire may not be as accommodating as his previous colleague boss had been. After setting up the Ritz security operation, and with a decade of service, Henri Paul now faced the possibility of being forced out by a new supervisor uneasy about his hotel security experience. Clearly, Ritz management was not taking care of Paul as a career professional.[6]

Another component of the Henri Paul enigma concerned the fact that most nations have an Embassy in Paris and many dignitaries and diplomats stay at the Ritz. Stories started to appear that Paul was in the employ of various "foreign and domestic" intelligence services. Then it was discovered he had one million francs [US$200,000–$250,000] spread between eighteen bank accounts in an attempt to disguise the fact. Al-Fayed would later make the claim Paul had spent at least three years working for British intelligence. Where he got this information, or if it is true, is unknown. Paul was also allegedly in contact with the Direction General de la Securite Exterieure [DGSE] - French Intelligence. So,

---

[6] The Hotel Ritz subsequently hired a former Scotland Yard Chief Superintendent John MacNamara. His background in criminal intelligence management and investigations was substantially different than Paul's Air Force Reserve security credentials.

Introduction

we were left with a feigned alcoholic dead man; with employment and big money surveillance concerns; ordered to violate multiple traffic laws; by a romantically aggravated boss in love with the world's foremost beautiful woman.

Henri Paul was uncertain about his future. He had to have been anxious about protecting his access to the Hotel Ritz time and date stamped video-monitoring system. He must have been concerned about his ability to generate good income by documenting high profile business people or foreign dignitary's arrivals and departures.

But all of a sudden, that night there was a positive side to the whole discordant affair. A rare opportunity to make a positive impression on the owner's son was at hand. In the wee hours of August 31, 1997, it would have been impossible for any driver to presume to caution a provoked Dodi Al-Fayed about safe driving on nearly deserted streets. As characterized by French Union Official Claude Luc:

> "If one of the Fayeds gives you an order, you follow it. No questions asked."[xxvi]

Whatever his prospects, Security Chief Henri Paul was illegally behind the wheel again. He was laid to rest in Lorient, France on September 20, 1997. Father Léon Théraud gave the sermon at Sainte Therese Church.

* * *

On Saturday night, now Sunday morning August 31, a physically aggressive horde of stalkarazzi and other onlookers, estimated at approximately 130 people, jockeyed for position at the front door of the Hotel Ritz Paris. Diana Frances Spencer and her boyfriend Dodi, son of Egyptian born multi-millionaire Mohammad Al-Fayed, needed a second car to exit the hotel's back entrance. Because of the paparazzi, a front door - back door scheme had been set-up for their return to Dodi's apartment. Dodi would take Diana out the back leaving his personal Range Rover in front as a decoy.

McMoneagle – Car is parked on the right side of the road (right side driving) which would rule out England,

Princess Diana Introduction

Bahamas, Hong Kong, Japan, etc. It is night and it is dark. The time for this event is current, probably 1985 to 1997. I will try and bring that down to a shorter period later.

The tag on the limo is elongated, with letters and numbers--which is a European style of tag (License 688 LTV 75). My sense is that there may actually be two colors of tags on this car, or that it has inter-changeable tags, which are changed, dependent upon where it is being operated. One is yellow with black lettering; the other is white with black lettering. It may be that there are two different colored tags on the car simultaneously—one color on one end, one color on the other.

This is a superb surveillance example. The yellow license with black lettering was on the rear bumper. As it turned out, the color license designated a private car. The white tag is a "for hire" vehicle. From this the reader can gather the type of information available through remote viewing should this car have been driving a foreign dignitary.[7]

After some hallway discussion, Ritz chauffeur's Philippe Dourneau and Jean-Francois Musa drove two decoy vehicles to the hotel's front door. The night was clear. The temperature was 77 degrees [25C]. Their engines were revved up as Dodi and Diana hurried out the back door at 12:20 a.m.

Diana's last few minutes on earth were now inexorably caught-up in the emotional web of her incensed boyfriend and his driver's employment needs. Some paparazzi across the Rue Cabman observed them as Trevor, Diana, and then Dodi came through the turnstile and got into the Mercedes. Henri Paul pulled out and the chase was on.

McMoneagle - Believe the car is the main focus of this target. The man [Paul] may also be of interest.... I believe this target has to do with an accident that probably occurred either in the very late night hours or possibly very early morning hours. Traffic is very light and the streets are very quiet. Get a

---

[7] In Foreign Relations, these plates could indicate a restricted territory vehicle. If unauthorized, remote viewers could be tasked on who issued both types of plates to the same party. This inquiry would remain secret, while perhaps unmasking a corrupt government official, or a mole in the host country's bureaucracy.

Introduction

sense that there are few cars about, in a place which is usually crawling with cars.

The Mercedes is moving very fast from what apparently is a northwest...direction. Have a sense that it goes over an overpass or cloverleaf kind of interchange which then drops straight down into a tunnel.

Associated Press
A back door security camera photograph time stamped 12:19 a.m. just before they departed. It shows Henri Paul (left) conversing with Dodi and Diana with Trevor Rees-Jones in the background

The car traveled toward the Seine River's westbound express street referred to as the Cours la Reine. Then they entered the Alexander III & Invalides Tunnel Bridge. The tunnel is 330 meters (361 yards) long.

McMoneagle - It [Mercedes] **then exits the tunnel and covers a large curve of open road which enters another tunnel like area, only this second tunnel is not enclosed completely. Have a sense of concrete tiers on one side... Vehicle is moving very quickly, perhaps in the neighborhood of approximately 100 MPH** [162 km/h], **maybe even a bit faster (in some spurts or straightaways).**[8]

In my opinion, the driver was driving way beyond the speeds that would have been comfortable for the place and

---

[8] The curve in the road is 480 meters [.3 miles] in front of the next tunnel, which provides an acceleration area. But with a subsequent curve and dip, it was not possible to negotiate that section of highway at high speed.

Princess Diana Introduction

time. I believe he was well trained as a driver but not for the place or speed at which he was driving. I have a sense the driver was doing his damnedest to carry out the instructions of those he was carrying, but was operating at speeds and conditions that even he was never really trained to drive within. I think he was the professional here and was being egged on by the passengers.[9]

These sessions took place approximately ninety days before the release of the official fifty-two page report entitled, *Accident de Passage Souterrain de l'Alma. Paris Dimanche 31 Aout 1997, 0h25. Propostition d'Analyse Scientific et Technique. Synthese et Conclusions.* French Engineer Jean Pietri had been commissioned to write an engineering crash analysis, which went on to verify this earlier remote viewing material.

The distance from the first tunnel to the Pont de l'Alma tunnel is 1.2 kilometers (.75 mile). The speed limit is 30 mph (48km). It is here that published accounts differ. Apparently, three people witnessed four to six paparazzi motorcycles attempting to pull alongside the speeding Mercedes. Other accounts say the paparazzi were a quarter of a mile behind when the Mercedes entered the tunnel. In either event, it was all futile. Notified by telephone, reporters had already assembled at Dodi's apartment entrance, million-dollar picture in mind.

McMoneagle – The Mercedes pulls out to pass a slower moving vehicle at a point in the road where the road ahead rises upward to a secondary overpass. Because of the rise in the road, the driver can't see on-coming traffic in time to avoid it, specifically at this speed.

The final report showed this was correct. French accident investigator Jean Pietri subsequently stated:

"To our surprise, we observed that the field of view is extremely limited. Passing cars disappear from sight well before they actually enter the tunnel because the descending road is obscured by a retaining wall. To the left the field of vision is blocked by a row of trees."[xxvii]

---

[9] McMoneagle was correct on this detail. Paul had attended special driving courses in Stuttgart, Germany from 1988 through 1993, receiving high marks, and Dodi knew this.

Introduction

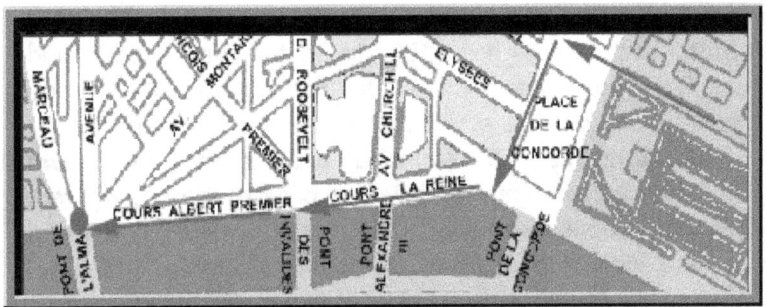

A view of their route along the Seine River. The arrow (top right corner) points the direct route to Fayed's apartment.

About 40 meters (44 yards) in front of the tunnel the Mercedes hit a gap in the pavement, which further destabilized control. As the car passed a white Fiat Uno at break neck speed Henri Paul saw another car dead ahead.

McMoneagle – I believe he sees an on-coming car which appears to be some kind of a black or dark green sedan. I want to say Citreon, but I'm really not sure. Probably a smaller two door car, two passengers; get a sense of dark green or green-black combination, which could mean a green car (body) **and black** (trim).[10]

Mohammad Medjahdi was driving a Citroen BX with his girlfriend Souad in the tunnel ahead of the Fiat Uno.

McMoneagle – Dodi's last words - Have a fleeting sense that he [Paul] is being ordered to go faster and to do more erratic things, to avoid something. He is essentially being ordered to do what he is doing.

To avoid the on-coming traffic, the Mercedes driver swerves hard to the right and catches the small car he is passing [Fiat Uno] **with his rear bumper. Car that was passed was hit. As a result, the Mercedes slews around left, just misses the on-coming car, which** [it] **has just passed, and the driver then begins to over-correct his steering.**

Months after these sessions, French engineers confirmed the Mercedes did nick the Fiat Uno and over corrected to the right.

---

[10] McMoneagle was obviously in the car looking through the Mercedes windshield. The use of "oncoming" describes the overtaking of cars. It does not refer to opposite direction traffic flow.

Princess Diana Introduction

Some tail light/head light debris was found.[11] Engineers estimated that if the Mercedes was going 100 miles per hour the debris would have rolled sixteen meters (52.5 feet). That hit took place outside the tunnel and it is here the 18.9m (62ft) tire skid mark begins.

McMoneagle - The Mercedes hits the side to left slews across and hits the right, then swings back to the left, where it catches what appears to be a concrete tier or pier (#13 pillar) **of some kind, concrete pilasters, or some kind of upright** (steel reinforced) **concrete dividers, which it hits nearly head on.**

At 12:24 a.m., there was an explosion sound in the tunnel. The subsequent engineering report confirmed Henri Paul's last evasive actions was viewed correctly. Various eyewitnesses recounted the collision. "Gaelle L., 40, a production assistant stated:

"*At that moment, in the opposite lane, we saw a large car approaching at high speed. This car swerved to the left, then went back to the right and crashed into the wall with its horn blaring. I should note that in front of this car, there was another, smaller car.*"[xxviii]

McMoneagle - The Mercedes apparently nearly goes end over end rear to front, but doesn't quite make it [over the top], **instead spinning twice and winds up pointing back in the direction it was coming from.**

The car spinning 1 1/2 times remains unconfirmed. But there was enough inertia for the car to have spun 540 degrees when the rear wheels were off the ground. The impact was so hard that the forward roof area was crushed down to the level of the driver's knees. This is further substantiated by the fact Diana was found facing backward in the back seat, which would not have happened with a simple 180-degree turn. *Newsweek Magazine* reported French police estimated the car had slowed down to 85 mph at the point of impact.[xxix]

The entire trip had taken about four minutes. Trevor Rees-Jones could only recall the Fiat Uno.

---

[11] The tail light pieces found in the tunnel belonged to a Fiat Uno manufactured between May 1983, and September 1989 by Seima Italiana. The white paint chips were called Bianco Corfu. When found, the car had been repainted.

Introduction

Rees-Jones: *"It seems to me there was one white car with a boot which opened at the back [hatch back], and three doors but I don't remember anything else."*ˣˣˣ

He did not leave the hospital until October 4 - thirty-four days later. Aware Henri Paul did not have alcohol in his system we sought clarification to research about drugs in his blood stream.

McMoneagle - Substance review - I believe if the driver had drugs in his system, whatever kind they were, they were not there by his own hand. I have this sort of strange feeling that he was not deliberately drugged to hurt anyone, but maybe he was drugged to get the car stopped along the route for the "photographers" to get their shots. In other words, his control was tampered with by outside influences. I don't think he was drunk, possibly drugged, but not drunk.

Here the research came full circle. The paparazzi had attempted to slow the Hotel Ritz airport shuttle vehicles earlier that afternoon on the drive from the airport. Once it was discovered, Henri Paul had been an informant for domestic as well as foreign intelligence services we went back to McMoneagle. Could the British government have been involved?

McMoneagle - My sense is that MI-5 (British Intelligence) **did not put the stuff in his drink. However, one might contemplate that if he [Paul] was willing to take money from foreign intelligence operatives, he most certainly would have been open to taking money from the Paparazzi. Maybe they were hedging their bets by having a small "drink" with him in the bar before he started driving.**

And what of the high carbon dioxide levels in Dodi's blood stream? Since this viewing, there were reports of a carbon monoxide suicide in Paris that night.

McMoneagle - You have to open your perception a little bit here. He did not have to have any evidence of CO_2 in his blood for them to find CO_2 in a blood sample. You only have to switch the samples at the hospital, the morgue, or the lab. Or, pay off the guy who is doing the tests. You could also conceivably rig the test equipment. Also, there are drugs, which will give a false reading as well.

Princess Diana Introduction

His being drugged enough to cause the accident could be attributed to a drug delivered in coffee, tea, or a drink beforehand. It could also have been sprayed on the inner edge of his door handle (driver's side), painted on the steering wheel, or inside a pair of driving gloves. He could have been shot with a needle delivery system, or pricked his hand, finger, leg, or almost any part of his anatomy on a delivery system getting into or out of the car. It can even be filmed across the pages of a book or map that he might have used to check directions on.

If he had a normal medical condition, they could have used a drug, which reacts violently with the drugs he is already taking for the medical condition. In which case they would either get false readings, or evidence of his medicinal drug, plus some other known drug which would not have been viewed as culprit in the event, simply because no one recognized the possible expected reaction. You also have problems with drugs which are binary in nature and can be delivered in two sittings, so to speak, where the victim gets part A in the morning with breakfast, part B in the evening with dinner, both of which are enzymes and when mixed... cause everything from hallucinogenic behavior, to strokes.

Now we turned to what Dodi and Diana where thinking.

McMoneagle - Back seat travelers - **MAJOR PROBLEM:** When I try to access others who might have been in the car, I get heavy [analytic] overlay and interference as relates to Diana's death in France. My head fills up with all kinds of motorcycles, and all kinds of news... that was being broadcast about the incident. I believe there were at least two others in this target car, but digging anything out of the overlay is completely impossible.

There is a sense from the people in the back seat that they want to be alone together, but again, I then get overwhelmed with all the Princess Diana stuff... and it all runs together. So, I can't begin to tell where [the] overlay begins and real data ends. Would prefer to say nothing.

It's rather interesting. I actually have not opened the envelope nor have a clue as to the real target here; but I am being overwhelmed with overlay which is self-generated. Must

Introduction

have been a lot of energy around the Princess Diana stuff. Better to just go no further with it. End of Session.
An abrupt stop, on a then well-known topic, due to analytic overlay. This is a graphic demonstration of the differences between military remote viewers, storefront psychics or hot lines. The media had been saturated with Princess Diana coverage in the period between the accident and this tasking. A psychic hot-liner would have been able to talk and bill without end about what they "saw". One Operation Star Gate military remote viewer commented, "There are many "*psychics*" who have taken this type of gibberish to a finely honed skill."[xxxi] But, when McMoneagle got to the Mercedes back seat, he stopped the session. In intelligence work when you are not sure of your viewing, you must say so. Any elaboration is unethical as in life and death situations, military viewers must stay grounded in the target's realities.

Analytic Overlay [AOL] is terminology within the Controlled Remote Viewing [CRV] protocols developed by Mr. Ingo Swann for the U.S. Military Intelligence Community at the Stanford Research Institute as they developed the nomenclature. AOL can generate bad data. So, can anything be done about it?

McMoneagle - Military research - There were a number of experiments which were run to examine whether or not a remote viewer can identify "AOL" while in session. We found that it could be rarely demonstrated. Most viewers are unable to tell (accurately or consistently) when something was AOL or when it wasn't, while in session.

Facts are; Evidence produced within labs suggests that no one methodology is capable of identifying and extinguishing AOL any better than another over the long haul.

There have been significant runs of very low AOL or displays of almost no AOL which have been done by individual remote viewers. So, there are indications that some people might have a talent for producing less AOL than others. But it does not appear to be method driven since it doesn't hold up in testing across all remote viewers using the same method.

So, why should identifying AOL be important??? It is important because, while you are attempting to learn remote viewing (regardless of method), it makes you think about how

Princess Diana Introduction

and why you are "thinking" about something. It is meant to reduce the speed by which you automatically jump to a conclusion. It also supports the structure and keeps one within it (at least until one becomes proficient enough to no longer need it.)

After the impact, eyewitnesses saw a motorcycle 30 to 40 meters behind the Mercedes slow down to observe the accident and then accelerate away from the scene. At 12:26 a.m., the Paris Fire Department - Sapeurs-Pompiers Unit - received a cell phone call from a Gaelle who was in the tunnel. Within one minute another call went out to the "service d'aid medicale urgente" (SAMU) - a civilian emergency medical service.

Inside the wreck, Diana and bodyguard Trevor Rees-Jones were still alive. One eye witness said he heard a woman crying loudly. One of the paparazzi, Romuald Rat, indicated Diana was conscious. He claimed he told her to stay calm; that help was on the way. She remained in the car...

Aftermath

Now pandemonium broke out as the Press fought each other to get the new million dollar shot. One photographer leaned into the car to reposition Dodi's corpse for a posed picture. Someone else came with video equipment. Within five minutes, Police Officers Lion Gagliardone and Sebastien Dorzee plowed through the crowd to the car. The police report stated:

"*I observe the occupants in the vehicle are in a very grave state. I immediately repeat the call for aid and request police reinforcements, being unable to contain the photographers and aid the wounded.*"[xxxii]

Officer Dorzee: "*I finally got to the vehicle... The rear passenger (Diana) was also alive... She seemed to be in better shape* (than Rees-Jones). *However, blood flowed from her mouth and nose. There was a deep gash on her forehead. She murmured in English, but I didn't understand what she said. Perhaps 'My God!*"[xxxiii]

Ultimately, six paparazzi were held in connection with the frenzy in the tunnel. They were arrested on suspicion of involuntary homicide and failure to assist persons in danger. Excepting the 24-

Introduction

year-old Romuald Rat, 40 was the average age of those arrested. Twenty film rolls were confiscated providing police with the photographic evidence they needed to confirm each man's activities that night. Three paparazzi got away.

There are no Miranda rights in France, nor is there a right to call an attorney. French authorities can hold a suspect for forty-eight hours before the prisoner must be formally charged or set free. However, it is certain Henri Paul did not have to be drunk or drugged to have had an accident at that speed.

The former Princess of Wales, Diana Spencer, arrived at the Hospital de la Pitie-Salpetriere at 2:00 a.m. She was pronounced dead at 4:00 a.m. It was then she attempted to contact her son William in Scotland. "William had had a difficult night sleep and had woken many times. That morning he had known, he said, that something awful was going to happen."[xxxiv] When he was told of his mother's death he said, "*I knew something was wrong. I kept waking up all night.*"[xxxv]

At 5:00 p.m. Prince Charles, 48, flew into Villacoublay military airfield outside Paris from Aberdeen, Scotland with Diana's sisters Sarah McCorquodale and Jane Fellows. "Diana's sisters spent most of the flight to Paris in tears. The Prince was controlled but clearly very shaken."[xxxvi] By 5:40 p.m. he was greeted at the hospital by the French President and Mrs. Jacque Chirac (1995-2007). Charles was led into a room with his two ex-sisters-in-laws where Diana lay in a coffin. He asked to be alone with the body for a moment. When he came out his eyes were red. The accident was 368 days after the finalization of their divorce.

Diana's coffin, draped in the Royal Standard's yellow and maroon, was flown home by an honor guard in a British Royal Air Force BAe146 military aircraft to Northolt Air Force Base in England. She was then taken to the Chapel Royal at Saint James Place.

Undertaken by Levertons, her September 6 funeral was the largest in England since the death of former Prime Minister and Nobel Literature Prize winner Winston Churchill [1874-1965]. After the morning funeral, it was reported a million people lined the route as the body was taken from London's Westminster Abby. Different accounts estimated two to three billion people watched the day's events as the car traveled the seventy-five miles to Althorpe House.

Princess Diana Introduction

Later that afternoon her body was laid to rest on a 1,254 sq. meter (13,500sqft) island called The Oval in a lake on the Spencer's ancestral grounds. The four hundred-year-old estate was then partially turned into a tourist attraction.

On September 9, 1997, the week after Diana was buried the Al-Fayed attorney filed civil law suits against the French periodicals *France-Dimanche* and *Paris-Match*. The complaint specified invasion of privacy with willful and wanton reckless endangerment when helicoptering "stalkerazzi" got too close over the Fayed's villa in St. Tropez. But, for the Hotel Ritz, the question became who bears responsibility for the accident? Before 1997 was out, the Fayed, Spencer, Rees-Jones and Paul families had all filed papers to be made civil parties to the investigation. Under French law, this allows them to investigate the case file and participate in any damage awards. And as for the Paparazzi's fate:

"*In accordance with articles 175, 176 and 177 of the Code of Penal Procedure; The examining magistrates find that there is no case to answer in the case of the state versus the above named [Photographers].*"[xxxvii]

In July of 2004, after the planning, funding and construction were completed, Queen Elizabeth II personally opened the Princess of Wales Memorial Fountain in the southwest corner of London's fashionable Hyde Park.

Then, in April 2008, after a three year investigation costing $7.3 million ($8.7million/2018), a six month long British inquest report was released which included the testimony of 278 witnesses with more than 600 exhibits generating an 832 page report stating:

"*Our conclusion is that, on the evidence available at this time, there was no conspiracy to murder any of the occupants of the car,*" Lord Stevens of Kirkwhelpington, who led the inquiry, told reporters as he presented his findings here. "*This was a tragic accident.*"[xxxviii]

In September of 2012, the French magazine <u>Closer</u> published long distance paparazzi photographs of Diana's eldest son's wife Kate Middleton sunbathing topless while at the Queen's nephew, Lord Linley's, French chateau. A publically released statement on behalf of the Duke and Duchess said: "*The incident is*

Introduction

reminiscent of the worst excesses of the press and paparazzi during the life of Diana, Princess of Wales, and all the more upsetting to The Duke and Duchess for being so."

And as for the need to use remote viewing protocols:

McMoneagle - Pick whatever method you intend to pursue and stick to it like glue. AOL (Analytic Overlay) **is a fact of life and this will always be so. Those of you who can eventually see your way to controlling your inner-driven or more personalized prejudice while internally processing, will probably improve somewhat in reducing AOLs, but AOLs will never entirely go away.**

CRV (Controlled Remote Viewing) **is a "method" derived from a method the military used while attempting to "train" people to understand both protocol as well as what is going on in a remote viewer's head (such as processing or the lack thereof). It was also very specifically designed to "preclude" things from being done out of ignorance (during the RV session) that might impact on/or otherwise prevent the act of successful psychic functioning from taking place; in other words, insure that RV could be replicated and would work more times than not.**

I would add that formal testing in the SRI Lab showed that regardless of technique or methodology utilized, most viewers were unable to consistently identify AOLs when asked to identify them prior to feedback. I have to say most, because "a couple viewers" were able to do so during significant runs--but this is inherently talent based and not the general or common rule. I remind you all of what is termed the "AH-HA". If it were not for the Ah-ha's, there would not have been a program. At the end of the road, almost anything is right when you have finally come to understand that it is an inherent part of our nature and then you just simply can do it.

Princess Diana Introduction

References

[i] McMoneagle, Joseph W., *Remote Viewing Secrets – A Handbook*; Hampton Roads Publishing Company, Inc. 2000 p. xv
[ii] McMoneagle, Joseph W., *The Stargate Chronicles*; Hampton Roads Publishing Company, Inc. 2002 p. 182
[iii] Simmons, Simone, *Diana – The Secret Years* with Susan Hill; Ballantine Books 1998 p.120
[iv] Delorm, Rene, *Diana & Dodi - A Love Story - By the Butler Who Saw Their Romance Blossom*, with Barry Fox and Nadine Taylor; Tallfellow Press 1998, p.144
[v] Anderson, Christopher, *The Day Diana Died;* William Morrow and Company 1998 p.114
[vi] Anderson; p.113
[vii] Delorm; p.154
[viii] ibid; p.154
[ix] The Learning Channel Presentation - *Princess Diana*; A Fulcrum Production; a Granada Presentation for ITV 1998; hereafter referred to as *TLC*
[x] Delorm; p.155
[xi] Anderson; p.99
[xii] ibid; p.166
[xiii] Sancton, Thomas and Scott MacLeod, *Death of a Princess - The Investigation*; St. Martin's Press 1998 p.157
[xiv] Delorm; p.157
[xv] ibid; p.158
[xvi] Spoto, Donald, *Diana - The Last Year;*; Harmony Books 1997 p. 171
[xvii] Sanction; p.158-9
[xviii] TLC - Mohammed Al-Fayed interview
[xix] Junor, Penny, *Charles - Victim or Villain*; Harper Collins Publishers 1998; p.18
[xx] Sanction; p.167
[xxi] Final Report - Paris Prosecutor's Office; Head of the Prosecution Department at Courts of the First Instance; Examining Magistrates Hervé Stephan and Christine Devidal
[xxii] *TLC* - documentary information
[xxiii] *TLC* - interview with Dr. Martin Skinner.
[xxiv] Anderson; p.191
[xxv] Interview with Mohammed Al Fayed as per his internet site address: www.alfayed.com/indexie4.html, as published to the Internet on October 25, 1998
[xxvi] Spoto; p.172
[xxvii] Sanction; p 251
[xxviii] ibid; p. 6
[xxix] *Newsweek* Magazine; September 8, 1997; p. 33
[xxx] ibid; p. 241
[xxxi] Buchanan, Lyn, *The Seventh Sense*, Paraview Pocket Books, 2003, p. 190
[xxxii] Sanction; p. 17
[xxxiii] ibid; p.17 - 18
[xxxiv] Junor; p. 20
[xxxv] Spoto; p.180
[xxxvi] Junor; p. 22
[xxxvii] French Final Accident Report – Conclusionary Statement section
[xxxviii] Lyall, Sarah; <u>New York Times</u>; December 15, 2008

Part II

What you are about to read is the Remote Viewing Data the Intelligence Community would have received had they tasked this event in the interest of the People of the United States of America.

Evidential Details

"The worst term of all is "psychic." No stable definition has ever been established for it, and there are great hazards in attempting to utilize a term which has not much in the way of an agreed-upon definition.
Supporters do assume that it refers to extraordinary, non-normal (paranormal) activities of mind. But skeptics assume it refers to illusion, derangement and a variety of non- normal or abnormal clinical psychopathologies."

> R E M O T E - V I E W I N G - One Of The Superpowers Of The Human Bio-Mind;.
> Remote Viewing and its Conceptual Nomenclature Problems by Ingo Swann (09Jan96)

"We tried a lot of things. Like I always tell everyone, we "improved" on the Ingo (Swann) method a thousand times in a thousand ways. But our bottom line always had to be accuracy, so we had to keep track of the improvements. Most of those times, the resulting data showed that the end result of our "improvements" was to have the accuracy drop down and down and down. Those things which proved over time to work, we kept. Ingo will be the first to tell you that what we did and taught to new people coming into the unit wasn't his "pure" method. The minute someone would come back from Ingo's training, we would try to see if there were some way to make what they had learned work better in a military/political/espionage setting. Some things did work, and they are now incorporated into the "military" method which passes for the Ingo Swann method."

> E-mail from former Operation Stargate Data Base Manager Lyn Buchanan correspondence - 7/29/98

Evidential Details

R.M.S. *Titanic*

The *Titanic*'s Triangular Fortune

O Helmsman, turn thy wheel! Will no surmise
Cleave through the midnight drear?
No warning of the horrible surprise
Reach thine unconscious ear?
She rushed upon her ruin. Not a flash
Broke up the waiting dark;
Dully through wind and sea one awful crash
Sounded, with none to mark.

Excerpted from 'A Tryst' - *Poems of Celia Thaxter*; 1874
A *Titanic* premonition thirty-eight years before the disaster.

Copyright 1997 All Rights Reserved

The Lookout's Secret

The sinking of the *unsinkable* Royal Mail Ship *Titanic* - "How was it possible?" There has always been something captivating about a large community of innocent people terrorized by the realization their whole family could not escape a death at sea that bewitches the collective consciousness far beyond 1912. Except for the American Challenger Space Shuttle disaster of 1986, the *Titanic* looms as the 20th Century's most significant transportation catastrophe. This is because the impact of that much simultaneous slow death is hard to imagine.

Library of Congress

The discovery of *Titanic* 12,600 feet (2.38 miles/3,840 meters) below the ocean's surface in 1985, and the movie of 1997, widened interest in what may be the best example of confidence in the face of the elements. The lack of adequate lifeboats stemming from an outdated 1894 regulation doomed the last two hours of *Titanic's* 4.5 service days. These events have helped to create historical societies in more than one country simply because its stories, as well its dimensions, are legendary.

Launched from ship builder Harlan & Wolff's slip 3, *Titanic* required a crew of 892. Along with her sister ships, *Olympic* and

Evidential Details

Britannic, she was the second of three stupendous vessels built in virtually identical fashion in Belfast, Northern Ireland. At 882 feet 9 inches (269m), the ship's length was just 5 meters shy of three American football fields. With a width of 92.5 feet (28.2m) the ship's gross tonnage of 46,328 tons. Begun in 1909, she cost the huge price of £1.75 million equaling £99,855,000 in 2008, or an estimated US$ 485,295,300.

As tall as a 17 story building, with steam funnels 22 feet (6.7m) in diameter, even today the ship would be a sight to see. With her three million rivets, a larger passenger ship would not be built until the *Queen Mary* in 1934. *Titanic* was longer and heavier than any of the World War II aircraft carriers a third of a century later. Even 80 years later America's massive Forrestal Class nuclear aircraft carriers, seeing service in the 1991 Persian Gulf War, were only 16% longer. From stem to stern, it was a ten minute, four-block hike, over her miles of decks. One can imagine the impact this vessel had on nineteenth century Irish shipwrights.

Previously, the largest ships in the water were Cunard Line's 30,000-ton vessels the *Lusitania* and *Mauritania*. Axiomatic to the disaster was that *Mauritania* held the record for fastest Trans-Atlantic crossing with an average speed of 27.4 knots.[i] In a combined Trans-Atlantic passenger and parcels business equaling one million fares by 1905,[1] the stakes were high to image as a luxuriously fast carrier. These new ships were vital to the now high flying White Star Line because they were locked into a North Atlantic trade struggle against Cunard who had been in business, in one form or another since 1839.

The *Titanic* story is an inconceivable mix of thousands of human circumstances. People with hopes for a fresh start in America now trapped with the realization of their family's impending

---

[1] The British Board of Trade Assistant Secretary, and head of Marine Department, Sir Walter J. Howell testified at the British Disaster Hearings that 73 lives had been lost out of 3.75 million passengers in the 10 year period from 1892-1901. Over the next 10 years only 9 passengers had been killed out of 6 million fares. Between 1892 and 1912 there had been 25 accidents among the 32,000 transatlantic crossings. This meant passengers had a .07812% probability of a death from an accident at sea. This progressive record of excellence explains why authorities were complacent in 1912 when these technologically advanced, wireless equipped, double-hulled, compartmentalized ships came on line.

The Lookout's Secret

doom. Through the intervening century, many books and magazine articles have been written, as well as very popular movies retelling the night's events. And while there may be slight reinterpretations of known events, much of Twentieth Century *Titanic* text is based on previous source material. But as Peter Padfield points out in *The Titanic and the Californian*:

The myths which had started as newspaper reports or survivors' tales and later as Court judgments became accepted, and have been repeated authoritatively but often inaccurately in a host of books down to the present day.[ii]

Clearly, History, and the public, was not in need of another *Titanic* rehash. But a final unmasking of its mysteries using a thoroughly tested military intelligence capability, was completely different. This then is an effort to solve the ship's final mysteries while contributing new material or reinterpreting previous material such as can be demonstrated. Two separate target envelops were presented. Afterwards, follow-up questions were submitted. One area that was reviewed was the ship's provisioning.

McMoneagle - Actual provisioning of the ship, for its initial voyage, occurred over a couple of month's period of time. They began provisioning of non-perishable items during the month of February 1912. **Staples were completely loaded by the middle of March. Perishables were loaded in the final week prior to departure. The actual loading of the infirmary supplies took place between the 3rd - 6th...**[2] **This was supervised by the ship's Doctor** (Surgeon William O'Loughlin) **and his first assistant...** (Dr. J. Edward Simpson).

Provisions for the infirmary came from the same suppliers that provided support to the two largest hospitals within the city (Southampton) **and were delivered by horse drawn vans. I see them as being dark green with white pin striping. The emblem on the van was a modification of the medical Caduceus, superimposed over a small Red Cross emblem.**

---

[2] Correspondence with *Titanic* shipbuilders Harlan and Wolff of March 3, 1997, stated: *"The Titanic had her basic stores such as lubricating oil, ropes deck fittings etc. and enough coal for the voyage to Southampton loaded in Belfast."*

Evidential Details

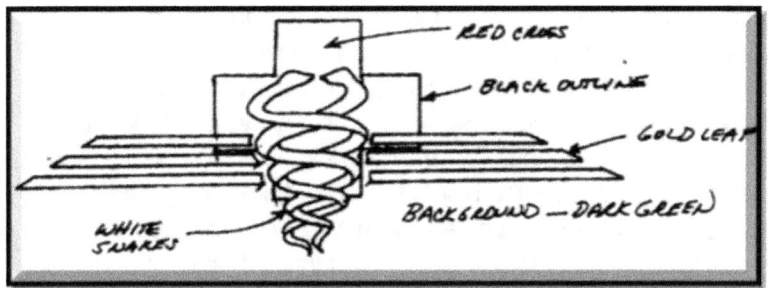

McMoneagle RV Art – Evidential Details ©1997
    Remote viewing surveillance illustration of the medical caduceus on the horse drawn green van that delivered the infirmary supplies to *Titanic*.

In London, on Thursday April 11, 1912, the British Parliament presented Prime Minister Herbert Henry Asquith with the Irish Home Rule Bill. That day R.M.S. *Titanic* put out from Roche's Point, Queenstown, Ireland, at 1:30 p.m. Before leaving the ship took aboard the last 13 crew members "lucky" enough to be hired for her maiden voyage.

Ultimately Captain Edward John Smith's men would power up all but four of her 29 boilers driving two reciprocating engines generating 30,000 horsepower enabling a propeller speed of 78-80 revolutions per minute.[iii] *Titanic* also sported a low pressure Parsons Naval turbine making practicable management's desire to pursue the Trans-Atlantic speed record in an era before commercial flight. These engines could approach 55,000 horsepower.

As the two 23-foot (9.75m) propellers and the 16-foot (4.8m) center blade started to churn, this most gargantuan ocean liner made its way into the open sea. With an empty test voyage top speed of 23.5 knots, *Titanic* went on to plunge headlong into a known ice field some 400 miles south southeast of Cape Race, Newfoundland at about 22.5 knots. She struck a medium size iceberg at 11:40 p.m. on April 14, 1912 consigning up to 1,523 people to death two and one half hours later, sinking at 2:18 a.m.[3]

For this target we began at the cutting edge. The *Titanic's* crow's nest is located high up in front of the ship's bridge. It is a

---

[3] It is speculated that if the iceberg rose 100 feet above the surface of the water it's below water draft would have been 600 feet bringing its weight to approximately 1,000,000 lbs. (453,592k). The berg was actually closer to 60 feet tall.

The Lookout's Secret

round, open, half-high iron platform fitted around a four foot diameter mast about 90 feet (27.5m) above the waterline (see page 51 forward mast). That night Lookouts George Symons and Archie Jewell were relieved when their shift ended at 10:00 p.m.

The new lookouts were Frederick Fleet who was responsible for the ship from the point of the bow back along the left side of the ship - the Port side. And Reginald Robinson Lee who was responsible for the ship's right or Starboard side. In the last moments *Titanic* was maneuvered so the ice struck on Lee's side. Regulations required two men in the crow's nest at all time.[4]

This evening there was reason for concern. At 11:40 a.m., *Titanic* had received an ice warning from the steamship *Caronia*. Again at 1:40 p.m. a wireless message was received from the steamship *Baltic,* and just five minutes later from the German liner *Amerika*. Then at 7:30 p.m., *Titanic* picked up ice hazard communications between the ships *California* and *Antillia*. And next came a warning from the merchant vessel *Meseba*. This is the fabled message the wireless men failed to deliver to the bridge.

McMoneagle - The men on the deck had severe night vision limitations. I feel that everyone on watch, as well as the First Officer, knew there was ice in the vicinity, as they were told by someone -- probably another passing ship earlier in the evening. There were three men in the forecastle and two men to Starboard and Port along the forward railings, with communication phones.

Racing at approximately 38 feet per second, the ship's forward ice observations were now critical to the outcome of the voyage. And the crow's nest light shielding was the best for looking forward into the moonless starlit horizon.

Questions have focused on how far forward the lookouts should have been able to see. Using 92 feet (28m) as the crow's nest "eye height" to the horizon, experts estimate the lookout's field of view would have extended 11.2 nautical miles. But with an ice-

---

[4] Fleet and Lee belonged to the category of "Specialized Lookout" and were paid 5 shillings more than the standard monthly pay of 5 Pounds. Their eyes had not been tested for five years and no post disaster eye test was administered even though a testing inquiry was made during the British Hearings.

Evidential Details

berg 60 feet (18m) tall, the first viewable distance is extended to 20.3 nautical miles (23.4 miles/37.6 kilometers) in daylight.

Oddly, the ocean was so still that night that Officers remarked one would only see waters this calm once in a whole career at sea. These freakish circumstances ensured there would be none of the normal whitecap wake action against the icebergs to make them visible from a greater distance.

But even without whitecap action or moonlight, *Titanic's* Officers calculated the lookouts should detect a pyramidal object on the horizon with ample time to alter course. In the dark, *"At a speed of 21.5 knots the berg should have been visible for the better part of an hour* (56 minutes) *prior to the collision."*[iv] Until these sessions, fog on the water had also been a controversy.

McMoneagle - Both men were on duty and in the crow's nest. I perceive the crow's nest as being just ten or twelve feet higher than the bridge and well forward of the bridge. Perhaps half way up the foredeck mast. From this vantage point I do not see a clear view of the area extending outward from the bow of the ship for a distance of about two hundred fifty feet. But outside that distance, from the ship's hull, there is a clear view of the surrounding ocean.

In the post disaster wrongful death lawsuit of Ryan vs. Oceanic Steamship Navigation Company (White Star Line's parent company) - the Précis Law Report stated:

"During his (Second Officer Lightoller's) *watch the captain came on the bridge at five minutes to 9 and stayed there for half an hour. They had a conversation. The captain's first remark was that it was very cold. He spoke generally about the weather. They discussed the question of ice. They knew they were soon entering the reported area, and they agreed that they would be able to see ice three or four miles away."*[v]

This safety margin was considered adequate to maintain speed.

But now the crow's nest responsibility had evolved from a forward looking position to a front line ice defense team. It was vitally important everything was in order as the men peered into the pitch black wind without binoculars.

The Lookout's Secret

McMoneagle – They were called from the upper deck (front of the bridge) by a second officer (Charles Lightoller) who informed them that ice was reported in the vicinity. They should be more alert. I believe that the same officer gave permission for one of them to temporarily leave the crow's nest for five or so minutes...

Permission to leave the crow's nest - after the ship was in the ice field! This was completely unknown in *Titanic* literature. That anyone gave permission for a lookout to leave his station became the first time this had used as a research premise. So, were there any evidential details?

First, we had to confirm that information was even communicated from the bridge to the crow's nest. Michigan Senator William Alden Smith chaired the U.S. Senate *Titanic* Disaster Subcommittee hearings in 1912, and did much of the questioning. In the U.S. Senate Hearings Quartermaster Robert Hitchens, 30, testified:

Hitchens - "...I heard the second officer (Lightoller) repeat to Mr. Moody, the sixth officer, to speak through the telephone, warning the lookout men in the crow's nest to keep a sharp lookout for small ice until daylight and pass the word along to the other lookout men." Third Officer, Herbert John Pitman, corroborated that these instructions had been passed along.

But could we confirm who received this call? *Titanic* crow's nest lookout Archie Jewell testified in the British Disaster Hearings.
British Question 17 - "Now do you remember when you were on your watch, from 8 to 10, any message coming to you about ice?
Jewell – "Yes, about 9.30 (p.m.).
18 - "What was the message?
Jewell – "To keep a sharp look-out for all ice, big and small."
19 - "How did the message come to you?
Jewell – "On the telephone; we have a telephone in the crow's nest.
20 - "That was telephoned up to the crow's-nest, and where was the telephone from?
Jewell – "From the bridge.
21 - "Then it would be the Officer on the bridge who would tele-

Evidential Details

phone to you?
Jewell – "Yes.
22 - "Do you happen to know who it was - which Officer it was?
Jewell – "I could not say. I think the Second Officer (Lightoller) was on watch at the time.
24 - "And after you got that message until you went off duty, did you keep a sharp look-out?
Jewell – "Yes, and passed the word along.
26 - (*The Commissioner.*) "What do you mean by "passed the word along" - to keep a sharp look-out for ice?
Jewell – "To the other look-out.
240. - "You stated in answer to the Solicitor-General, that when your watch was finished, your watch finishing I think at 10, you passed on to the two men who succeeded you the information you had got?
Jewell – "Yes, that was my orders from the bridge.
243 - "Is it usual for a man on the lookout - is it part of his duty to pass the word along in these circumstances?
Jewell – "Yes.

Officer Lightoller's shift also ended as lookouts Fleet and Lee climbed up into the nest. Would they corroborate Lightoller's information had word been passed on to them? Regarding this detail Senator Smith questioned Frederick Fleet:
Smith - "Had you been especially directed to look carefully?
Fleet - "Yes, sir.
Smith - "By whom?
Fleet - "By the mates we relieved; by the other two lookout men.
Smith - "Were you told to do so by Officer Murdoch?
Fleet - "No, sir. We got our order from Mr. Lightoller, and passed it on to the lookouts as they get relieved.
Smith - "Mr. Lightoller gave the order to your mates?
Fleet - "And they passed it on to us.
Smith: "Is that usual?
Fleet - "Yes, sir; as we get relieved we pass it on to the other men.
Smith - "If any orders come in the meantime to you, you pass them on?
Fleet - "To the next two men

The Lookout's Secret

Specialized Lookout Frederick Fleet, 25, (1887 – 1965) saw ice, telephoned the wheelhouse, and rang the crow's nest alarm bell single-handedly.

At 10:00 p.m. First Officer William McMaster Murdock replaced Officer Lightoller. Unknown to history is that Lightoller's permission to leave the crow's nest had also been passed along with the ice warning to the next shift.

McMoneagle - Officer Murdoch - The man at the helm, when the event took place, is taller than the Captain. His Number One. Angular face, very tanned, with a square jaw. He is cleanly shaven and wearing a dark uniform suit, which is probably blue. He has unusual eyes, gray or hazel, weighs about 160 pounds, is at least five feet, eleven inches tall - - maybe six feet even. He is approximately 45 - 48 years of age. He is ultimately responsible for the collision, even though he was controlling the boat according to the Captain's instructions.

So, did either of the lookouts leave the crow's nest during their shift? This remote view was originally targeted to determine where and how the Captain died. What brought us to a second *Titanic* viewing was what McMoneagle viewed in the ship's crow's nest just before the impact.

Evidential Details

McMoneagle – There was also a man in the crow's nest forward of the first stack. His location afforded the best view, since he was not hindered by all the light shining through the windows. (Author's underlining)

In what seemed like a remote viewing 'miss', we stumbled across a major new event in *Titanic* history. Lookouts Fred Fleet and Reginald Robinson Lee both swore they were in the crow's nest as the ice approached. But if true why did McMoneagle only view "...*a man in the crow's nest...*"?

It has been pointed out that as the iceberg came into view, "...without consulting his colleague, Frederick Fleet suddenly reached across and sounded the death-knell of the *Titanic*..."[vi] He then telephoned the wheelhouse. Nobody disputes Fleet sounded both alarms. But strangely, historians had to accept that if Reginald Lee was in the crow's nest he took no action regarding an iceberg impact on his side of the ship.

While not properly interpreted, *Titanic's* lookouts left a series of reactions and covering acts that would corroborate what really happened. Subsequent research revealed a White Star Line courtroom cover-up including phony claims of disability, management intimidation of employees and an incomplete subpoena.

Evidential Detail – Lookout Silence

The lookouts were a tight knit group who worked two hours on four hours off around the clock. That there was good communication between the lookouts has been established. But oddly, neither Fleet nor Lee passed along any information to the next lookouts after the impact.

Evidence of this came in the British Hearings. When next shift lookout Alfred Hogg[5] was questioned about the sighting of the vessel *Californian*, he made a broader statement reflecting on Fleet and Lee's refusal to pass anything along after the collision.
British Question 17559 - "When you went to relieve them at 12 o'clock was anything said to you then?

---

[5] George Alfred Hogg, 29, had 13 years experience as a Quartermaster and was a Bosun before taking the position of specialized lookout on *Titanic*.

The Lookout's Secret

Alfred Hogg - "Nothing was passed on to me <u>at all</u> then."

At this point the ship had come to a stop and by midnight was listing approximately five degrees forward to starboard. When Officer Lightoller issued his ice warning he knew the men regarded it as their duty to pass it along. So it seemed that after a collision at sea, a co-worker would ask, "*Hey, what happened? Any new instructions?*"

But shaken, neither Fleet nor Lee passed anything on about what was to become the defining moment in their lives. Lookout Hogg could have testified no information was passed along. But he chose to emphasize nothing was passed on "*at all.*" For some reason Fleet and Lee had fallen silent about crow's nest impact circumstances with their colleagues. There was good reason for this. Both men were apprehensive. A high speed forward impact, on their watch, did not bode well for their futures.

Evidential Detail - Crow's Nest Motion

As events developed, there emerged a consistent effort to divert attention from what happened in the crow's nest at impact. An example is that there is an absence in *Titanic* literature about the crow's nest motion. The fact that the hull moved is not in contention among passengers. So were there any evidential motion details?

From Toronto, a former Major in the Canadian Militia and sailor, Arthur Peuchen, 53, testified in the U.S. Senate Hearings.

Peuchen - "...I had only reached my room and was starting to undress when I felt as though a heavy wave had struck our ship. She quivered under it somewhat. If there had been a running sea I would simply have thought it was an unusual wave which had struck the boat; but knowing that it was a calm night and that it was an unusual thing to occur on a calm night, I immediately put my overcoat on and went up on deck.

Later Major Peuchen reinforced the idea:

Senator Smith - "You say when the impact occurred, the ship shuddered?

Peuchen - "When the impact occurred, describing it I would say it

Evidential Details

would be like a wave striking it, a very heavy wave.

Senator William Alden Smith was born in Dowagiac, Cass County, Michigan in 1859. He studied law and was admitted to the bar in 1883. Elected as a Republican to the 54th Congress, he served from March, 1895 until he was elected to the Senate starting with the January, 1907 session. He served as a Senator until March 1919 and was Chairman of the *Titanic* Disaster Subcommittee. Senator Smith died in Grand Rapids, Michigan in October, 1932 at the age of 73.

Library of Congress

Upon impact, everyone in the First Class Smoking Lounge stood up from their tables and some men moved quickly out to the deck railing. Down below (boiler room) Fireman George Beauchamp indicated the impact was like a roar of thunder and Greaser Thomas Ranger said the "jar" had lifted them off their feet. The impact was adequate to shift enough coal down below to momentarily trap a coal trimmer named Cavell.

Hoping to continue their careers at White Star Line, the Officers all minimized the effects of the "jolt". But *Titanic's* collision can be likened to a school bus hitting a street curb on the right front wheel. While significant for an ant on top a hood ornament shaped like a pencil, the collision would not seem substantial to the passengers toward the rear.

Testimony confirmed there were substantial differences in perception between passengers three blocks back inside the ship, and the crow's nest platform 90 some feet above the water line abreast of the impact point.

The Lookout's Secret

Unfortunately, our mathematical modeling efforts were hampered because of an impact pivot point requirement. The fact the ship was raised slightly before sliding down the side of the ice also hindered a water line center of gravity determination. But whatever the arithmetic it is physically impossible the crow's nest did not move.

McMoneagle – Crow's Nest Motion - The list was what I would term 'heavy'. My perception is the crow's nest probably shifted to Starboard approximately twenty-five feet (7.6m), then rocked back to Port, then less to Starboard, etc...

It is not too difficult to visualize Fleet hanging on during the powerfully lifting tilt to Port, then moving meters sideways to and then down in five to ten seconds. But like so much else surrounding crow's nest activity, this would have invited comparative "*what was it like*" anecdotal interest.

Neither man ever remarked about his carnival ride encounter with the berg except to deny it. And yet it should be one of *Titanic's* very few humorous asides. Fleet testified he thought the ship had a "close shave" with the ice. But the bottom line was that neither man shared the same experience and talk was risky.

Evidential Detail - Witness Tampering

Upon arrival in New York, Managing Director J. Bruce Ismay became fixed on getting certain crew members out of the United States. This was deemed so important that U.S. Marshals wired a halt to the *RMS Lapland* and sent a tugboat to New York's Sandy Hook harbor before the ship got out of U.S. waters. Customs Agents boarded and removed five subpoenaed crewmen. Quartermaster Hitchens was among them. But, the most important man present, Reginald Robinson Lee, was omitted from that subpoena.

With all documentation at the bottom of the Atlantic, hapless American officials had to rely on ship's management to identify the surviving crew positions as they considered whom to call. No information could be found regarding who "helped" investigators draw up the summons. But the fact Lookout Lee and Helmsman Hitchens were on the getaway boat betrays who management thought was sensitive. It was decided port side Frederick

Evidential Details

Fleet would to do all the talking for the starboard side of the boat.

Born in Benson, Oxfordshire, this is a younger Royal Navy Paymaster picture of the Starboard lookout Reginald Robinson Lee (1870 -1913/1929?). He first went to sea in 1887 and had over 15 year's seaman's experience in addition to his 14 years in the Royal Navy. Reliable, he had transferred in from the RMS Olympic on April 6. As the ice side lookout, he successfully dodged the American Hearings. After the British Hearings, he resigned but was summoned back to court for an Irish lawsuit. Concerned about more court action, he abbreviated his name and dropped from sight. He granted no interviews, left no known memoir or diary and there is no mention of *Titanic* on his grave stone. There are two versions of his death in two places in different decades.

Royal Navy

This was so well suppressed that it was not until after the hearings were moved from New York to Washington D.C. that it was even known who was in the crow's nest. Senator Smith asked:
Smith - "Did Lee survive this wreck, or was he drowned?
Fleet - "He is one that survived it.
When Senator Smith wondered why an absolutely crucial witness like Lee had not been subpoenaed Fleet, knowing full well Lee had sailed for England, said:
Fleet - "I do not know where Lee is. He got detained in New York."
In the British Hearings lookout Archie Jewell testified:
British Question 34 – "Do you know whether Lee has given evidence in New York?
Jewell – "I do not know. He has been kept back.
Until now, the reason why was unknown

Evidential Detail – Testimony - Frederick Fleet

The evidential details also include nervous, stay on script,

The Lookout's Secret

sworn testimony. Managing Director J. Bruce Ismay first made statements in New York's Waldorf Astoria Hotel East Room. He would then be called to testify at the Senate Hearings in Washington D.C. Ismay would then have to testify in the British Disaster Hearings and then again in a civil case. Fearing this eventuality, it became extremely important that White Star Line employees say nothing that contradicted his testimony.

Line Management's "see no evil - speak no evil" pressure can be observed when Frederick Fleet came before American Hearings. He was a specialized lookout charged with distance evaluations. But his coaching became obvious when Senator Smith asked a simple question about the crow's nest elevation.

Smith – "Can you tell how high above the boat deck that is?
Fleet – "I have no idea.
Smith – "Can you tell how high above the crow's nest the mast-head is?
Fleet – "No, sir.
Smith - "Do you know how far you were above the bridge?
Fleet – "I am no hand at guessing.
Smith - "I do not want you to guess; but, if you know, I would like to have you tell.
Fleet – "I have no idea.
Senator Fletcher - (*Democrat, Florida*) "You hardly mean that; you have some idea?
Fleet – "No; I do not.
Fletcher - "You know whether it was a thousand feet or two hundred?

Fleet did not respond to Senator Fletcher turning toward Smith for the next question. It was clear distance questions were considered off limits. But not wanting to appear ridiculous Fleet finally slipped up and revealed he could evaluate distances.

Smith - "The forecastle head is how high above the water line?
Fleet - "Fifty feet I should say.
Smith - "About 50 feet?
Fleet - "Yes
Smith - "So that black mass, when it finally struck the boat, turned out to be 50 feet above the water?

Evidential Details

Fleet - "About 50 or 60.
Smith - "Fifty or sixty feet above the water?
Fleet - "Yes.
  Referring to the ship's torturously slow curve away from the ice, Frederick Fleet was again asked to make a distance evaluation.
Smith - "But you saw the course altered? And the iceberg struck the ship at what point?
Fleet - "On the starboard bow, just before the foremast.
Smith - "How far would that be from the bow's end?
Fleet - "From the stem?
Smith - "From the stem.
Fleet - "About 20 feet.
Smith - "About 20 feet back from the stem?
Fleet - "From the stem to where she hit.
  It was now obvious Fleet had could judge distances. So instead, he became unable to judge ships speed or evaluate time.
Smith - "Can you not indicate, in any way, the length of time that lapsed between the time that you first gave this information by telephone and by bell to the bridge officer and the time the boat struck the iceberg?
Fleet – "I could not tell you, sir.
Smith - "You cannot say?
Fleet – "No, sir.
Smith – (Disgusted) "You cannot say whether it was five minutes or an hour?
Fleet – "I could not say, sir.
Smith - "How large an object was this when you first saw it?
Fleet – "It was not very large when I first saw it.
Smith - "How large was it?
Fleet – "I have no idea of distances or spaces.
  Of the six specialized lookouts, Fleet emerged with the severest distance, space, speed and time disabilities. Obviously, this would have disqualified him from this type of duty. But Fleet did describe the iceberg's size during the approach.
Fleet - "When first sighted, (the) berg looked about as large as two tables put together, but kept getting larger as the ship approached.

The Lookout's Secret

And, "When alongside, a little higher than the forecastle head, which is about 50' above water.
Smith - "Did Lee and you talk over this black object that you saw?
Fleet – "Only in the crow's nest.
Smith - "What did you say about it? What did he say about it to you or what did you say about it to him?
Fleet - (Safely covering old ground) "Before I reported, I said, 'There is ice ahead', and then I put my hand over to the bell and rang it three times, and then I went to the phone.
Smith - (Wanting more about Lee) "What did he say?
Fleet - "He said nothing much.

It was untrue that these two only spoke about the impact in the crow's nest. We will learn exactly what was said in a moment. But this back and forth on distance disability continued. And again, Fleet slipped up and attempted to cover up when he estimated his lifeboat was one mile away when *Titanic* foundered. Homing in on this discrepancy:
Smith - "How are you able to fix that in your mind - that you were a mile from the *Titanic* in this small boat?
Fleet - (Looking for a way out) "I heard people talk about it.
Smith - "Was that your judgment, too?
Fleet - "I ain't got no judgment.
Smith - "I understand you to say you have no judgment of distances at all -
Fleet - (*interrupting*) "No more I haven't.
Smith - "...when I was asking you about the iceberg?
Fleet - "No more I have not.

It was obvious the two areas to be kept secret were distance to the iceberg and the time from sighting to impact. Fleet was uncooperative and management issued no instructions to provide useful information. But Senator Smith continued to press the lookout circumstances.
Smith - "Who sighted the black mass (iceberg) first?
Fleet - "I did.
Then catching himself Fleet said quickly:
Fleet - "I say I did, but I think he (Lee) was just as soon as me.
Unfortunately no one in the American Hearings asked why

Evidential Details

was there was no participation in alarm duties by the ice side lookout. Why weren't there at least shared duties if there were really two men present particularly when the phone was on Lee's side of the thick mast ladder tube?

With a ship destroying iceberg looming dead ahead, *Titanic* historians have routinely believed Lee stood back and watched Fleet come around the mast to Lee's side and call the wheelhouse while pulling the alarm bell cord. But some authors have been suspicious of Fleet's testimony. In *The Titanic - End of a Dream* clinical psychologist Wyn Craig Wade was on track. He provided a description that helps historians interpret the atmosphere of the proceedings.

"Fleet now appeared before the committee, nervous and pitifully attired. He clutched his worn-out cap in his hands which he periodically twisted during his testimony. Speaking in a thick cockney accent, Fleet was often difficult to understand and appeared to have just as much trouble comprehending the senator's questions. Chances were he was...frightfully anxious, which he concealed the only way he knew how.

Smith - How far away was this 'black mass' when you first saw it?
Fleet – I have no idea Sir.
The lookout began twisting his hat, silent and remote.
Smith – Did it impress you as serious?
Fleet – 'I reported it as soon as ever I seen it.' Fleet retorted with unexpected rancor.

"It was difficult to tell what was gnawing at Frederick Fleet. He was obviously intimidated by the proceedings, but Smith watched him continually looking off to the side at Officer Lightoller and (Managing Director) Ismay. Was he hiding something out of fear of reprisal from his employers?"[vii]

Months later, in the British Hearings, Frederick Fleet's attitude "came out as truculent, even paranoid" again. For some reason it appeared Fleet was being prompted as to how to testify. But in England he was protected by a powerful Maritime Union whose legal counsel was there to serve the men as opposed to get at the truth. So when talking about the possibility of haze on the water and his previous discussions with Second Officer Lightoller,

The Lookout's Secret

Fleet reacted to White Star Line Counsel Sir Robert Finlay:
Fleet - "Well I'm not going to tell him (Officer Lightoller) my business. It is my place in court to say...not him.

After a series of uncooperative answers a disgusted Chairman of the British Hearings the Right Honorable Lord Mersey, 72, (The Commissioner) finally stepped in over Legal Counsel and issued an admonishment.
Lord Mersey - (Exasperated) "You really do not understand. This gentleman (Finlay) is not trying to get around you at all.
Fleet - "But some of them are, though.
Lord Mersey - (Disgusted) "They are not. I can see you think most of us are, but we are not.

Fleet was obviously concerned about someone "getting around" him, which implies cover-up. Defiant rather than cooperative toward the end of his questioning he said:
Fleet - "Is there any more likes to have a go at me?"[viii]

In the back of Fleet's mind may have been a statement published by Horatio Bottomly in the British publication *John Bull*. "Someone ought to hang over this *Titanic* business. Sixteen hundred men and women have been murdered on the high seas."[ix] "Fleet was certainly an awkward and highly defensive, not to say paranoid, witness, obviously under enormous stress."[x] So, rather than saying, "The witness may step down", at the end of Fleet's testimony, the Commissioner had a comment.
Lord Mersey - (Conciliatory) "'I am very much obliged to you. I think you have given your evidence very well, although you seem to distrust us all.' Fleet's ordeal was over: any secret he was hiding remained hidden."[xi] - until McMoneagle was tasked.

So what about this defensive behavior? Psychiatrist Sigmund Freud was 56 at that time.
Freud - "Realistic anxiety strikes us as something very rational and intelligible. We may say...it is a reaction to the perception of an external danger – that is, of an injury which is expected and foreseen. On what occasions anxiety appears...will of course depend to large extent on the state of a person's knowledge and on his sense of power vis-à-vis the external world."[xii]

In the States Fleet knew he was powerless if unmasked.

Evidential Details

But, even with his time "disabilities," he wound up with a job for life at White Star Lines. As a result, he avoided the trenches of World War I twenty-eight months later. His steady employment continued through the Twenties and the darkest days of the 1930's Great Depression, even though management was fully aware of his sworn occupational disabilities.

It was not until White Star Line sold out to Cunard in 1934 that Fleet's management protection ended. And even though this company man should have been considered a valuable employee with over twenty-five years of insider knowledge of White Star Lines vessels, equipment, operations, and ports of call, Cunard released him within two years at age forty-seven. If Fleet was really a time and depth perception disabled employee why had he lasted so long when he was on the watch that sank *Titanic*?

Evidential Detail – Testimony - Reginald Robinson Lee

Titanic's details became even stranger when with starboard lookout R. R. Lee's British Hearings testimony. Once out of the States, he was coached on his upcoming testimony. Decisions were made: **1)** for him to emphasize haze on the water; **2)** that he had "disappeared" from sight in front of the four foot (1.2 meter) mast; **3)** that he too was unable to estimate speed or distance. His only testimony was given in London.

British Hearings Question 2611 – "Is it not also usual when you are in a fog or in a haze to slacken speed?
Lee – "Certainly.
2612 – "And speed on this occasion was not slackened?
Lee – "I could not tell you.
2613 – "You could not tell?
Lee – "No.

As we will see later, Lee's iceberg testimony was all fabricated. Imagine his stress when giving sworn testimony about something he never saw from a station in which he was absent.
Question 2435 - "You were on the starboard side of the crow's-nest, you told us?
Lee – (falsely) "Just at that time I happened to be right in front of the nest, because as the nest is semi-circular the telephone is in

the corner of the nest on the starboard side. My mate (Fleet) was telephoning from there, and I was standing in the front of the nest watching the boat.
2436 – "Do you mean you were standing just about amidships?
Lee – "Just about amidships in front of the nest (mast).
2441 – "Can you give us any idea of the (iceberg's) breadth? What did it look like? It was something which was above the forecastle?
Lee – "It was a dark mass that came through that haze and there was no white appearing until it was just close alongside the ship, and that was just a fringe at the top.
2442 - "It was a dark mass that appeared, you say?
Lee – "Through this haze, and as she moved away from it, there was just a white fringe along the top. That was the only white about it, until she passed by, and then you could see she was white; one side of it seemed to be black, and the other side seemed to be white. When I had a look at it going astern it appeared to be white.
2447 - "Quite right; that is where she hit, but can you tell us how far the iceberg was from you, this mass that you saw?
Lee – "It might have been half a mile or more; it might have been less; I could not give you the distance in that peculiar light.
2450 – "Did you see at all how much ice there was that fell on the forewell deck?
Lee – "I knew there was some there, because I saw it when I went on to the boat deck.
2451 – "You did not pay particular attention?
Lee – "No, I had something else to think about.

    Indeed he did. Lee was the only one who referred to a "peculiar light" and ice "coming through the haze", implying the haze was as tall as the berg. Fleet also testified about this haze:
British Question 17252 - "Was the haze on the waterline?
Fleet – "Yes.
17253 – "It prevented you from seeing the horizon clearly?
Fleet – "It was nothing to talk about.
17254 – "It was nothing much, apparently?
Fleet – "No.

    And so this next exchange fit right into this scenario.
Question 2601 – "How long were you on your last watch before

Evidential Details

you observed the haze?

Lee – "I think I answered that question before. Didn't you hear me answer that question before?

Mr. Scanlan - "I did not.

The Commissioner - "You must not whisper your answers. Speak up so that we can hear you.

2602 (*Mr. Scanlan.*) "How long had you been in the crow's-nest on your last watch?

Lee – (still focusing on the previous question) "It was not so hazy to begin with as it was when the accident occurred.

2605 (*Mr. Scanlan.*) "Were you not then of the opinion that the pressure of that haze made the passage dangerous?

Lee – (dodging) "I am not the Officer of the watch.

Mr. Scanlan - "I am not accusing you of that.

Lee – "That has nothing to do with me. I am not on the bridge. I am a look-out man, as I said before.

2608 – "You have often been in a fog, I daresay, in Atlantic passages?

Lee – "I am in a fog now.

He certainly was. Beleaguered, Lee was trying to make certain he made no mistakes that could open a can of worms resulting in imprisonment for perjury and possibly worse.

To protect White Star from speed negligence allegations Second Officer Lightoller claimed there was no fog. In *Titanic* literature there has always been this haze and fog controversy.

McMoneagle - There was surface fog, but it was fading in and out. I don't get a sense that there was solid fog, but I believe there were intermittent sections of heavy, nearly solid water-level fog which the ship sailed in and out of for a number of hours.

Oddly, during the thirty-six day British Hearings (May 2 - July 7, 1912), Reginald Robinson Lee focused on what he had not seen that night. Again a disgusted Lord Mersey, "...dismissed Lee's testimony altogether, saying it was inconsistent with everything else the court had heard. 'This man was trying to make excuses for not seeing the iceberg,' he Mersey said, which was surely true."[xiii]

The Lookout's Secret

The fact the British Hearings Chairman accused Lee of not seeing the iceberg is consistent with "a man" in the crow's nest. And while there was no proof that day, from the corporate point of view, Lee was relieved of further questions helping to prevent conflicts. No legitimate challenge was issued until these remote viewing sessions 85 years later.

But this was not all that Lee had to lie about.

British Question 2690 – "Is there an examination of the eyes before you are appointed look-out man at Southampton, or elsewhere?
Lee – "Yes.
2691 – "Who by?
Lee – "You go through the Board of Trade office.
2692 – "At Southampton?
Lee – "Yes.
2693 – "What doctor examined you?
Lee – "I do not know his name.
2694 - "A doctor did examine you at Southampton; did he particularly examine your eyes; did he test your sight?
Lee – "Yes.
2695 – "Do you swear that he tested your sight at Southampton at the Board of Trade Dock there; do you swear that?
Lee – "No.
2696 – "Let us be quite clear. You were examined by the Board of Trade doctor at the Southampton - is that so?
Lee – "I am not going to answer that.
2697 - (Lord Mersey - *The Commissioner.*) "What did you say? Were you examined at Southampton by a doctor?
Lee – "Yes, Sir, but not for eyesight though. He only just asked me - not a test to get a certificate so that I can prove it. There is a doctor's examination when you fall in.
2698 - "Were you asked about your eyesight?
Lee – "Not specially.

It took one last sequence of evidential details to clarify all the strange behavior in what should become a permanent revision in *Titanic* history.

Evidential Details

Evidential Detail - Fleet's Last Interview

In the summer of 1964, Frederick Fleet granted an interview to author Leslie Reade. From the day of the disaster, and for the rest of his life, Fleet upheld his Hearings testimony that two men were in the crow's nest at all times.

Now 76, Fleet spoke of events from over half a century ago. He would be dead in just over six months. As he spoke to Reade, Fleet accidentally revealed the reason for all the bizarre testimony in the Hearings. During this interview Fleet declared:

Fleet - "I said to Lee, '*You better go down, there's no sense the two of us being up here, if we strike.*' He didn't want to go. '*I can't do that,*' he (Lee) said. But I made him and he went down the ladder.

Surprised, Reade put the obvious question; was Fleet alone in the crow's nest. But then Fleet remembered this contradicted his 1912 testimony.

Fleet - "*No, he* (Lee) *climbed up back. We was up there together.*

Remember, two men in the crow's nest is an absolutely iron clad part of *Titanic* history etched in stone for all time. Yet, as early as 1964, historians should have realized what really happened. The reason for their oversight is that author Leslie Reade failed to label his thoughts as opinionated when referring to one of the most significant *Titanic* revelations of all time. Regarding Fleet's one man in the crow's nest statement, Reade wrote: "*That also, was new, though not important...*"[xiv]

New though not important is an oxymoron! Nonetheless, Reade's disqualifier relegated Fleet's remark to obscurity for the rest of the 20th century. Without remote viewing, it may never have been interpreted properly.

The 17-year younger Frederick Fleet was not Reginald Robinson Lee's boss. So why, in the grips of the incredible human drama of the ships torturously slow turn away from the berg, would the ice side lookout suddenly take instructions to climb down the crow's nest ladder forcing Fleet to perform both alarm duties? Obviously there was every reason for Lee to stay and watch the iceberg approach on his side of the ship.

The Lookout's Secret

Assuming Lee was even agreeable to leave it is utterly inconceivable a lookout, charged with Starboard watch duties, would not wait another minute for the impact before departing. Clearly, no one would want to be accused of abandoning his post at a time like this if only for reporting duties. But even going so far as to suppose Lee did not care to witness the impact it did not make sense he would climb "*up back*" into the crow's nest once partially down the mast ladder.

Because of its historical significance, we wanted to be certain of our understanding and ask the reader to indulge a short analysis. The key components of Fleet's statement are:

1) The words "*if we strike*". This means the conversation took place between the sounding of the alarm and impact.

2) The "*...no sense the two of us being up here...*" is imprecise. It could refer to a face to face discussion in the crow's nest. But it also allows Lee to be anywhere within speaking distance. The only other place possible was inside the mast ladder tube as the ship's deck was too far down.

3) "*Up back*". Fleet stated he directed Lee to go down the ladder. But "*up back*" refers to the upward return of Lee. The mast ladder works is the only place "up - down" activity could take place. Fleet said there was, "*no sense in the two of us being up here*" because he was talking down the oval mast ladder tube entrance thus clarifying the variable in point two.

That he witnessed Reginald Robinson Lee's movement in and out of the crow's nest - as the ice approached - was Fleet's final statement. He disclosed it and then tried to cover it up.

But Fleet had not told Leslie Reade everything. And what made him seem even more candid was that his behavior became very guarded afterward. Concerning another question:

Leslie Reade - "Did you see the lights of another ship when you collided?

Fleet - "No, sir, I must tell the truth. There was no light.

With the implications of his *up back* statement, Fleet felt he must now reinforce his truthfulness. Sensing this, Reade's narrative now moved from *Titanic* to Fleet's conduct.

Reade - "He was emphatic about this, repeating it more than once,

Evidential Details

and pleadingly, as if begging to be believed, although no word of contradiction was put to him.[xv]

Over half a century after the event Fleet realized he had just let the "cat out of the bag" to an author. His nervousness in 1912 now made sense. For the first time, through the use of remote viewing, we are able to reconstruct a complete picture as regards the lookout's behavior.

In both Hearings, the lookouts were asked about the weather. And their answers were uniform.

Fleet - "No, sir. It is all open in the nest, sir.
Smith - "Was that a cold night - Sunday?
Fleet - "Yes, sir.
British Question RR Lee 2405 – "Was it cold?
Lee – "Very, freezing.
British Question GA Hogg 039 – "Was it cold?
Hogg – "It was bitter cold.
British Question RO Hitchens 105 – "You said it was pretty cold that night?
Hitchens – "Very intense cold, sir.

But except for temperature, we found no effort in *Titanic* literature to gauge crow's nest environmental factors. The air is always referred to as 32 degrees (0 C). Without data, a moderate Temperature-Humidity Index of 25 percent lowers the temperature to 28.3 degrees F (-4 C). But assuming the ocean winds were completely still, the ships forward progress created a 22.5 knot (26 mph) wind chill lowering the temperature to as cold as 6 degrees F (-14.4 C). The men had stood in this wind for 90 minutes.

Shift durations also changed as *Titanic* sailed through International time zones. The ship's clocks would be set back to indicate 12:00 midnight at 12:20 a.m. local time. So westbound, Fleet and Lee were due to bear this cold for an extra twenty minutes. Extra watch in this weather, explains Officer Lightoller's giving permission for one man to leave the crow's nest.

This was McMoneagle's second *Titanic* viewing. He was targeted at 11:30 p.m. ship's time and advised of the lookout's names to avoid confusion.

McMoneagle - 7 bells/11:30p.m. - When the ships bell

The Lookout's Secret

rang ...Lee temporarily left the crow's nest, via the ladder, and moved back toward and into the main deck galley of the ship. My sense is that this was agreed to between him and Fleet.

Fleet agreed to man the watch alone while Lee went to the forward galley to find something hot for them to drink. Lee was supposed to bring this hot drink for him and Fleet to share in the crow's nest. My sense is that it wasn't coffee. It was some sort of a heavy sweet dark tea. It was carried in a medium sized metal container made of tin, which had a large cork in the top and a cord for a handle. Lee was still in the forward galley when Fleet first sighted the iceberg from the crow's nest.

My sense is that he (Lee) was not alone, but he wasn't talking with anyone either. He was just one of a couple of people in the galley, and he was filling the tea carrier. I have a perception that the container, tea, etc., was dumped all over the place by him in his immediate reaction to the alarm. He left it all sitting on the counter in his haste to return to his post. He left immediately.

It is apparent Lee was not concerned about being seen. The earlier shift had probably gotten hot tea after Lightoller told them it was permitted. But this violation of regulations would have put management under intense legal pressure.

McMoneagle – ...the man in the crow's nest spotted the iceberg prior to the collision and called it down to the Wheel House with about a two - three minute warning. Insufficient time to turn the vessel. I believe Fleet did not see the iceberg until it was within 800 - 900 yards of the ship. Fleet began ringing his warning alarm as soon as he sighted the iceberg. But, it took almost 2-3 minutes for the First Officer to identify which side of the bow the ice was approaching from, as it appeared to be dead ahead.

Lee attempted to return immediately to the crow's nest when Fleet began ringing the alarm bell. However, I don't believe he ever actually made it back to the crow's nest itself. Lee was...about a third of the way up (to) the crow's nest when the ship actually struck the iceberg. The short but hard list to

Evidential Details

C Deck Galley

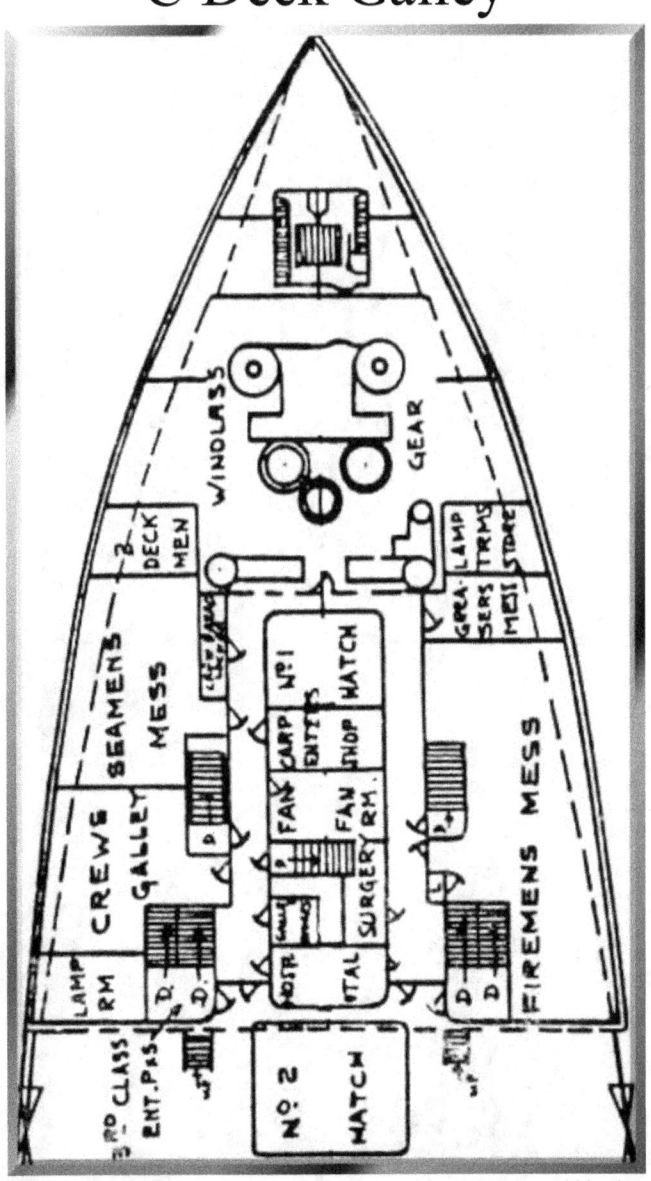

We searched the ship for a location lookouts could get hot tea within the narrow time constraint described by McMoneagle. In what seemed remarkable, the Crew's Galley and Mess hall appeared on the Portside of C-Deck (upper left).

The Lookout's Secret

Harlan & Wolff (Olympic)

With the C-Deck Mess down inside the ship's hull, left **(1)**; Lee made his way over to the mast ladder door underneath the forecastle deck **(2)**; and about 33% up inside the mast ladder tube to be in range of a conversation with Fleet **(3)**.

Evidential Details

the Starboard probably made it difficult for Lee to continue up the crow's nest ladder works. It would have been pretty violent to the guy in the crow's nest, but not so violent to the guy just beginning to climb. Both certainly would have been fighting to regain their feet.

Now we knew how and why but were there any evidential details? Was there even a seaman's galley located within running distance within the time frame of iceberg sighting to impact?

Amazingly, a deck analysis showed there was a crew's galley and mess hall forward on the Port side of C Deck. *Titanic's* ship builders Harlan & Wolff were contacted to review the time frame and distance from the seaman's galley to the mast ladder entrance. When asked about the route a sailor would most likely take the shipbuilders responded from Belfast, Northern Ireland:

Harlan & Wolff: *"It would depend or where the lookout was going (and) which staircase he would use but the most likely would be the port side as this placed him directly outside the door leading into the seamen's mess and galley."*[xvi]

When asked: "Take any able bodied seaman under 6 feet tall, is it possible to approximate how long it would it take to run from inside the C Deck crew's galley to the crow's nest ladder works inside the mast?"

Harlan & Wolff: *"Assuming he was expecting to go and was stood ready about 50 seconds is a safe assumption. The mast is in the centre or half breadth of the ship and the ladder is equidistant between the mast and the side shell."*[xvii]

Obviously, Lee was taken by surprise pouring hot liquid. Picture the astonished lookout having to stop the flow, jerk the canister aside and run. Unfortunately there are no official estimates of how long it takes to climb the mast ladder as this is a human coordination variable. And again a mathematical model is muddied by the fact Officer Murdock ordered the engines into full reverse which gradually slowed the ship down to 16 – 18 knots at impact.

McMoneagle - He probably made it in under a minute and a half. He was in a great hurry to join his friend in the masthead.

After running over to the mast and ducking through the

The Lookout's Secret

The sinking of the *unsinkable* Royal Mail Ship *Titanic* - "How was it possible?" There has always been something captivating about a large community of innocent people terrorized by the realization their whole family could not escape a death at sea that bewitches the collective consciousness far beyond 1912. Except for the American Challenger Space Shuttle disaster of 1986, the *Titanic* looms as the 20th Century's most significant transportation catastrophe. This is because the impact of that much simultaneous slow death is hard to imagine.

Library of Congress

The discovery of *Titanic* 12,600 feet (2.38 miles/3,840 meters) below the ocean's surface in 1985, and the movie of 1997, widened interest in what may be the best example of confidence in the face of the elements. The lack of adequate lifeboats stemming from an outdated 1894 regulation doomed the last two hours of *Titanic's* 4.5 service days. These events have helped to create historical societies in more than one country simply because its stories, as well its dimensions, are legendary.

Launched from ship builder Harlan & Wolff's slip 3, *Titanic* required a crew of 892. Along with her sister ships, *Olympic* and

Evidential Details

Murdoch's countermanding order makes it appear to be his mistake, which explains his subsequent suicide. In any event, this initial misdirection <u>snugged</u> the boat right up alongside the ice.

McMoneagle - The event is ushered in by what feels like an elongated shudder which runs through the boat, followed by an almost gentle listing to the port side. The boat heeled or listed in the direction or side facing the iceberg. There is not much sound accompanying the event, but I sense air horns on deck are blaring for some reason – an alarm or call to stations for the crew.

This "call to stations" is an example of remote auditory sensing. A bosun's pipe was sounded calling all hands to deck. The *Titanic's* largest ever triple-toned whistle sounded along with whistling steam release valves as the ship slowed to a halt. "It was deafening and impossible for anyone to be heard."[xviii]

McMoneagle – R.R. Lee – So, he abandoned the attempt and reported in to the wheelhouse/bridge. Fleet continued to ring the alarm bell for some time. My sense says about 5 minutes minimum. Then he abandoned the crow's nest himself, reporting in to a deck officer on the main deck just under the Bridge.

My sense is that it took only about eight minutes for everyone on board the ship to know...they had hit something, by the jolt and shudder that ran through the boat. However, most didn't know immediately that it was serious. There was considerable confusion at first on where to go. Most knew which decks the lifeboats were on, but no one knew which lifeboat was the one they should go to.

Now we understand why McMoneagle saw *a man* in the crow's nest and why Fleet sounded both alarms. But in 1912, this would have destroyed the lookouts. Unaware of Officer Murdoch's countermanding orders, imagine a Prosecutor's logic making the case that had both men been in the nest they "might" have seen the iceberg sooner. The sooner the alarm the sooner the evasive action. The sooner the evasive action the less damage to the hull. The less damage to the hull the fewer flooded compartments. The ship, and its 1523 dead, "quite possibly" could have been saved.

The Lookout's Secret

Given the fever of the times imagine the lookouts facing a loud badgering lawyer's mocking tone, "*So, you wanted hot tea did you?*" Both men could have been charged with Gross Criminal Negligence culminating in the largest single wrongful death in maritime history. And if that happened, the following information would have been brought forward to protect these Union men.

From a hospital interview First Class Saloon Steward Thomas Whiteley recounted a discussion he overheard from one of the lookouts in his lifeboat. The New York newspaper quoted:

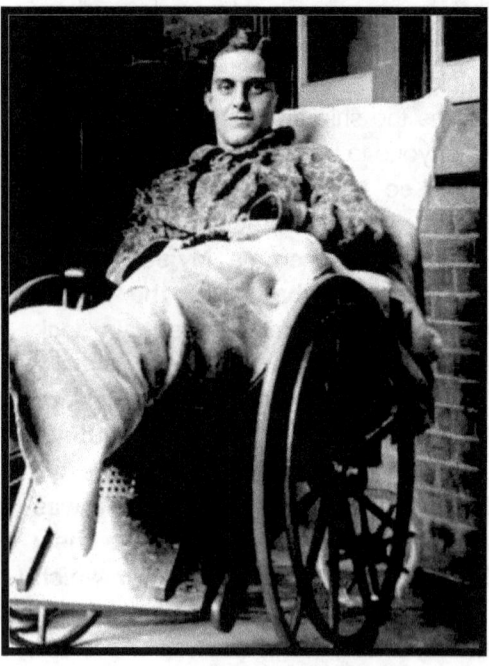

Thomas Whiteley recovering at St. Vincent's hospital in New York. His little known lifeboat recounting is history's last word on activities in the crow's nest just before Lee's untimely departure to the seaman's mess for hot tea.

Photographer Unknown

"*I heard one of them say,*" he said last night in the hospital, "*that at a quarter after eleven o'clock on Sunday night, about twenty-five minutes before the great ship struck the berg, that he (Lee) had told First Officer Murdock that he believed he had seen an iceberg. He said he was not certain, but that he saw the outline of something which he thought must be a berg. A short time later, the lookout said, he noticed what he thought was another mountain of ice. Again, he called the attention of the first officer to it.*

Evidential Details

A third time he saw something in the moonlight (starlight) which he felt certain was an iceberg. The air was cool and there were indications in his mind that there were bergs in the neighborhood. A third time he reported to the first officer (Murdoch) that he had seen an iceberg. This time, as I recall it, he did not say merely that he fancied he saw one, but that he had actually seen one. His words to the officer, as I remember them, were - 'I saw the iceberg. It was very large, and to me it looked black, or rather a dark gray instead of white.'"[xix]

Here Mr. Whiteley addressed the possibility of lookout negligence. As none of this talk was heard in Fleet's lifeboat 6, he had to be listening to Lee in boat 13. With the phone on his side of the crow's nest, Lee apparently called the bridge three times over the preceding 25 minutes making Fleet's call the fourth. Figuring the bridge was well warned and that it was the officer's responsibility to control the ship, Lee could nonetheless be accused of violating work rules when he left for the galley. But then he had permission – but only through the previous lookouts advice.

Moreover, the truth would have had devastating corporate repercussions. This disaster would be the modern equivalent of one airline sustaining five Boeing 747 jet crashes on the same night, killing 304 people each. What was at stake was the credibility of White Star Line as a safely managed carrier and thousands of jobs. The consistency of bizarre testimony, remote viewing results and subsequent human behavior now makes White Star management's shielding Reginald Robinson Lee from the American Hearings appear, perhaps, right minded.

Like Fleet, Lee lived out the rest of his life concerned about being unmasked. He may have also felt partially responsible for the death of all the passengers. And he may have been paid to disappear. In 1995, it was published that Reginald Robinson Lee, "...appears to have vanished into the mist of history...completely... even the painstaking and resourceful *Titanic* Societies, British and American, have found no trace of him."[xx]

McMoneagle - My perception is that Lee never went to sea again - certainly not to cross the Atlantic to America. I see him working on the docks in England. The specific place

The Lookout's Secret

appears to be mainly dealing with cargo, not passengers, although passengers certainly come in here as well. It is also one of the harbors which is nearly land locked, having only a narrow channel in and out to the sea. Lots of heavy industry, steel mills, railroad connections. My guess would be Liverpool, England. I do not believe he changed his name. He went by his second name as a worker, abbreviated to Rob Lee. I have a sense he died fairly early in life from a heart attack, probably a complication of heavy drinking. I believe he was 58 - 59 years of age when he died.

That time line puts Lee's date of death in 1928-29. In 1964, Fleet told author Leslie Reade:
Fleet - "Lee left White Star Line and worked for the Union-Castle where he served in the *Kenilworth Castle*. Said Fleet, "he died of drink many years ago.'"[xxi] But was it 35 or over 50 years ago?

Union-Castle

After the *Titanic* Hearings, Lee worked for the Union-Castle Mail Steamship Company Limited, London (Est. 1900). This rare picture of the *Kenilworth Castle* shows the 12, 975 dead weight ton vessel which was in operation from 1904 to 1936.

Here Fleet slipped again. He must have "known" Lee "died" in 1913. But he also knew Lee was not an alcoholic on the *Titanic* and that one year on from 1912 was insufficient time for a man to die from alcoholism. So this second quip, coupled with McMoneagle's information, brought on another new *Titanic* research trail. Lee's death needed to be finally established.

Reginald Robinson Lee left White Star Lines for reasons that are now obvious but never disclosed. What we do know is

Evidential Details

from June 20 to 26, 1913 Lee testified in a law suit known as the Ryan Case at the Royal Courts in the Strand, London. Here fresh testimony was introduced by the ship's surviving Officers. Also testifying were Frederick Fleet, George Hogg and radioman Harold Bride. The legal verdict for all time, found White Star Line negligent of wrongful death due to an excess of speed in a known ice field.

With this precedent, White Star was faced with hundreds of civil actions, or a massive class action lawsuit.[7] Management had lost employment control over the disaster's star witness, who would repeatedly be called to testify in every case on both sides of the Atlantic. There was great danger if Lee let his guard down on just one question, and so White Star thought it best that he disappear. Nor would Lee have wanted to go on "testifying." Plus his absence would lower a plaintiff's odds in court.

So Lee wound up "dead" in Portsmouth, England on Tuesday, August 5, 1913 just five weeks after the Ryan trial. Even if Lee was employed before the trial, his employment could not have been more than one year. Our research found the Union-Castle employee register confirmed Lee as an employee but the critical start and end dates, shown for all the other employees, were missing. And the Union-Castle records keeper refused to respond to our e-mail.

But someone was not on board with Lee's demise. In the Southampton Press, Lee's obituary death date is Tuesday, August 5, but his death certificate reads August 6. Then they got it into the weekend press of Friday, August 8, 1913 to run these word for word identical obituaries in the *Southern Daily Echo* and the *Hampshire Advertiser*.

Link with the *Titanic*:
Death of Look-Out Man at Southampton.[xxii]

"*A notable figure among the survivors of the Titanic <u>has been removed</u> by death at the Sailors' Home at Southampton on Tuesday of Reginald Robinson Lee, on whom an inquest was held*

---

[7] The Thomas Ryan case set a precedent for claims brought in the United States as well. Settled out of court in December, 1915 of the tens of millions sought only U.S. $663,000 ($16 million/2017) was shared among all U.S. claimants.

The Lookout's Secret

by the Borough Coroner (Mr. H. K. Pope) yesterday afternoon. The jury returned a verdict in accordance with the medical evidence."

The story goes that Lee checked into the Sailor's Home on Friday breathing heavily. He was last seen alive at 11:50 a.m. on the next Tuesday morning. For plausibility, his cause of death was pneumonia just like his father's.

But his removal, autopsy, contacting and seating of a coroner's inquest, testimony, verdict, reporter coverage, layout, printing and street distribution all happened - according to his death certificate dates - in the space of 48 hours. This was an impossible flurry of activity in a time before home telephone.

As part of a plan, it appears White Star Lines submitted the newspaper's obituary copy. Lee's may be the only English language bereavement notice proclaiming the deceased, *"has been removed."* But it provides a glimpse into their thinking.

R. R. Lee must have been considered a key White Star Line liability and measures were taken to prevent future court appearances. They may have told him that if the public found out, he would hang for leaving the crow's nest, but that he could avoid punishment by playing along with disappearing - permanently.

Lee would not have been on *Titanic's* maiden voyage if he was an alcoholic. And death by alcoholism takes years to develop. Now we had a McMoneagle/Fleet vs. the Death Certificate conundrum, with either pneumonia or alcoholism as the cause of Lee's untimely death. So it was time to go where other authors have not gone and take a look at Lee's burial circumstances.

His body is reportedly at the Highland Road Cemetery, Southsea, Portsmouth. Closed to new plots since 1956, the cemetery has a striking heritage and promotes its interns. The Friends of the Cemetery web site proclaims:

"Amongst those interred are many servicemen and women, including scores of Generals and Admirals as well as 8 holders of the Victoria Cross, as well as associates of Charles Dickens and even Royalty."[xxiii]

So it appeared, with this practice of keeping track of

Evidential Details

various dignitaries, it was odd there was no mention of the ice side lookout on the watch that sank *Titanic* even if it was just for an infamous interest factor. Lee was found relegated to third position on the "others" web page. Included was this notice:

> *"Please note: the former Adopt-a-Grave scheme has been terminated."*[xxiv]

More odd language. The "termination" of a "scheme", rather than the "discontinuance of a program", made it sound as if there was something wrong with Adopt-a-Grave. We presumed people had adopted Lee's grave and, given what we knew, it would be logical that this must not continue.

But in a £5 yearly donations environment, it would seem any organization would leverage this unique asset to include the worldwide, ever evolving, *Titanic* enthusiast trade. If promoted properly, Lee's membership draw could supersede any single "distinguished" grave. One could even consider a permanent RMS *Titanic* remembrance wall pasting donor's names up for a £25 contribution particularly during the 100th Anniversary. In our correspondence with the Friends of the Highland Road Cemetery office, we were cordially advised:

> *"William and Jane Sarah, the parents of R R Lee, and R R Lee are all in the same grave."*[xxv]

But triple level graves, with none cremated, is unusual. Unfortunately, the 1875 British Burial statutes then in force, were modified by the end of 2004 and jurisdiction transferred to the Ministry of Justice. With this new legal environment, our nineteenth century statute research was hampered, but we did confirm this practice was lawful during the Twentieth Century.

This grave would have been opened twice after Lee's father died in 1887. But, as expected if our scenario was correct, the church, the minister and any acquaintances that attended Lee's graveside eulogy went unrecorded. Again the Friends Office:

"There would have been a funeral service for RR Lee but there is

The Lookout's Secret

no report of it in the local paper for that year so I do not know who was in attendance."[xxvi]

Here was another anomaly - no church records - and the lack of normal obituary coverage. So, we contacted the Cemetery's Office. They responded:

"In this case the Highland Road records only show the date of burial, the plot details, the persons buried, their age and where they died. No other records were recorded for this individual."[xxvii]

Highland Road Cemetery triple level plot containing William (d.1887) Reginald (d. 1913?) and mother Jane Sarah (d.1920) The Plot is M Row 4, Grave# 11. There is a headstone and a curb surround. The poorly chiseled gravestone appears to have been sanded to obstruct easy reading allowing weather to smooth it more quickly.

Reproduced courtesy of www.Friendsofhighlandroadcemetery.org.uk

But for some reason the response began, *"In this case..."* which implies cases existed. So we asked about the church, the minister's name, etc., and if any of this information was retained for "distinguished" people.

"All our records are uniform, the extra data you have mentioned is not statutory and therefore we do not keep this detailed information."[xxviii]

Evidential Details

Not even for a decorated General, Admiral or historic Royalty? This was obviously not right, but stymied we moved on to the Coroner's Office. Unfortunately it turned out those documents were destroyed in the German blitz of 1941. In an e-mail, we inquired:

Q) *"Was 100% of all pre WWII Coroners documentation wiped out, or were some scattered remnants re-assembled in whatever form?"*
A) *"Apart from some September 1939 records that are with the County Council, all were destroyed. As you can imagine, you're not the first person to ask me about this."*[xxix]

So, the time line discrepancies, the lack of church records and standard newspaper coverage, the odd Adopt-a-Grave and newspaper write-up language, the lack of cemetery data, dual causes of death and death dates - coupled with a serious motive - still led to an inability to absolutely resolve Fleet's assertion without a grave site investigation. Which brings us to the bottom line. Would <u>you</u> order an exhumation based on a series of overwhelming evidential details derived from a decorated U.S. Military Intelligence remote viewer?

Once White Star lost the civil case, Lee's "death" was necessary to quash future subpoenas. With a fraudulent headstone, death certificate, and bogus inquest jury findings on the books, anyone could now "prove" Lee had been dead since 1913. So, where is Lee really buried?

McMoneagle - He is buried in one of the Liverpool cemetery plots, which is adjacent to a large stone church. There is a long walkway from the street leading to a stone archway. There is a small bell in the archway. There are twin towers, which are square and are not much taller than the center of the roofline. The towers are not very pointed. There are stained glass windows that go nearly from the ground to the ceiling along the side of the church. The stone is kind of a yellowish color (sandstone). **The graveyard is at a 90-degree right angle in the extreme front of the church.**

The Lookout's Secret

This was clearly not the Highland Road Cemetery. So what are the clues to Lee's gravesite location?
1) In Liverpool, not Southampton England;
2) Large yellowish stone church;
3) Long walkway from the street leading to a stone archway;
4) A small bell in the archway in 1929;
5) Square twin towers equally as high as the church roof line;
6) Stained glass windows from the ground to the ceiling along the side of the church;
7) Graveyard at a 90° right angle the church building
8) Lee's grave's location is in the extreme front of the church.

This church (likely Presbyterian) should not be difficult to locate unless it has been demolished. Either way the cemetery should still be there with a grave list. Someday someone will solve the riddle of R.R. Lee's grave. So what of Fleet?

McMoneagle - Fleet continued to be a sailor. He sailed out of England about three months after his arrival there, as a deck hand on one of the White Star sister ships (R.M.S. Olympic). I believe he stayed with the company until it went out of business, then continued his life as a sailor aboard other ships of like function.

Fleet did move from White Star Line to Cunard Line until he was let go in 1936. He then worked for *Titanic's* shipbuilders Harlan & Wolff retiring in 1955. Difficult to get along with in retirement, he took odd jobs including selling newspapers in Southampton while living with his wife at his brother-in-law's house. For safekeeping, he stuck to the story that the whole tragedy could have been avoided if binoculars had been in the crow's nest.

From the day of his birth, life never gave Fleet an even break. As an infant he was a Victorian era mistake. Wanting a fresh start, his mother gave the baby to his uncles and boarded a ship to the States with what was to become her American husband. Ironically, she is reputed to have gone to Springfield, M.A., the subsequent home town of the U.S. *Titanic* Historical Society just 140 miles (225km) from New York City.

She married, took his name, and is currently lost to history.

Evidential Details

Due to the massive publicity and public fascination, she may have read excerpts of her son's testimony in the newspaper. It would be interesting if the then fiftyish woman realized that the only U.S. Senate lookout testimony came from her infant son whose last name Fleet she should have remembered from 25 years ago.

Fleet had acted responsibility in the line of duty but it did not matter. Through no fault of his own, he was forced to live 3/4's of his life protecting forced perjury about the worst maritime disaster in history. Unhappy about this bad break, combined with his tough start in life, he became increasingly irascible. And even though a Union member, the Line was able to get rid of him eighteen years before it was time to retire.

On January 10, 1965 two weeks after his wife's sad Christmas death, Fleet hanged himself from a garden post in Fremantle, a Southampton suburb [Death Certificate DXZ 544157]. He was despondent because he could not get along with his brother-in-law. He was told to leave with no money and nowhere to go.

Destitute, he was buried in an unmarked pauper's grave at Hollybrook Cemetery in Shirley, Hamptonshire. In 1993, the U.S. *Titanic* Historical Society placed a headstone in his memory. He will be forever remembered as *Titanic's* port lookout who single-handedly sounded both alarms for an incident on starboard side.

* * *

The third man in this triangle was Helmsman Robert Hitchens, a twenty-nine year old from Cornwall. He was relieved by Quartermaster Perkis at 12:23 a.m. and went to help Fleet load lifeboat six. From the revelations in the 2010 Patten book, we learned why Hitchens post disaster fortunes are also suspicious. On duty since 8 p.m. that night, he had control of the wheel when Officer Murdock gave the order to whirl it to its utmost extreme.

Based on Ms. Patten's information, Hitchens originally turned the wheel in the wrong direction losing precious seconds. But even before her book, there had always been suspicions about his role. "Less speculative is (the U.S. *Titanic* Historical Society's then Vice President George) Behe's account of an alleged confession, that he (Hitchens) had been offered a well-paid job in

The Lookout's Secret

return for suppressing certain unspecified events on the bridge of the *Titanic*. He became harbourmaster at Cape Town, South Africa..."ˣˣˣ

Key witness Wheelhouse Helmsman Robert Hitchens (1882-1940).

Research confirmed Hitchens did leave England to visit his brother in Johannesburg, South Africa. It appears he worked in Cape Town as a Masters, Mates and Pilots type Harbormaster going out to greet incoming vessels. Henry Blum wrote to Hitchen's friend Thomas Garvey:

"...the "harbourmaster" who came out to meet the boat was Hitchens, although harbourmasters do not routinely meet ships but are in charge of overall port traffic and tariffs. Blum claimed he and Hitchens had a talk in which he was allegedly told that Hitchens had been set up in South Africa in return for his secrecy regarding Titanic."

Concerned with Fleet, but touching on Hitchens in e-mail correspondence with George Behe, I asked if he thought Fleet had been, "Taken care of in some way, shape or form."

George Behe - "If Fleet's friend (who told of Fleet's "confession") was indeed telling the truth my answer would be "yes." Naturally though we'll never know the truth of the matter -- although the fact that Hitchens was said to have received an independent (but

Evidential Details

identical) bribe lends added weight to the possibility." [8]

It is pretty obvious management considered Hitchens, Fleet and Lee as problematic. And in a catastrophe this size, bribery probably seemed reasonable. But more compelling was that to obstruct litigation, White Star Line wanted Hitchens clear out of Great Britain. And with Lee "dead" and Fleet's "don't know anything about anything" testimony providing employment for life, we observe the trianglularized activities. With McMoneagle supplying the last puzzle pieces, *Titanic's* secrets fell into place.

The preponderance of the Evidential Details support the idea there was only one man in the crow's nest at impact. So, with Leslie Read's interview freely available, we found it interesting both lookouts obviously scared perjury was still "History" as this material was brought forward. It now seems clear *Titanic* historians would be remiss to talk in terms of two men in the crow's nest after 11:30 p.m. that night.

Senator Smith - "Tell the committee what you did after you left the crow's nest that night.

Fleet - "I went down below and I found there was nobody down there, and the quartermaster (Hitchens) come down and said we were all wanted on the bridge.

McMoneagle – My sense is that both Fleet as well as Lee acted as message couriers between this officer, the bridge, and other parts of the ship from that point on, or at least until about 12:55 to 1:00 a.m. Both men were ordered to report to their life boat stations at that time.

An exact picture is difficult to detail but, dead in the water, Ship's Command ordered a lookout impact report and dispatched Hitchens to bring the lookouts to the bridge. At this point Lee, Fleet and Hitchens probably spoke among themselves on a deck below the bridge. And from all indications, this encounter turned ugly. Hitchens may have attempted to shift blame to the lookouts because something was said that angered Fleet. Hitchens may have said he was aware Lee was absent from the crow's nest.

---

[8] Mr. Behe referred to a "confession" by one of Frederick Fleet's friends claiming a payoff took place to contain testimony about ice sightings that were relayed to the Bridge from the crow's nest as was verified by Mr. Whiteley's statement.

The Lookout's Secret

Their first night in New York the crew was sequestered onboard the *RMS Celtic* by security guards. That day meetings took place between Director Ismay and the crew. They were given orders not to talk to anyone under the threat of immediate termination without money to get home. But one reporter did gain access and his article appeared in the April 23, 1912 New York Times entitled, *Sealing the Lips of Titanic's Crew.*

Three decks down, in the mess hall, this reporter asked Fleet what had happened. At first, he refused to respond as were his orders. But then:

"Not a word," replied Fleet, *"except that when I get me hands on that guy what gave out the story about me---him as was running the wheel, as he said---why, when I get him he'll be lucky to know if his name's Hitchins or Hawkins. He said he saw me in the crow's nest. Now, there was a cabin in between and he saw nothing of me at all, nothing at all, and what's more, he ain't one of us."*[xxxi]

From this, we can conclude the lookouts were told to stick together. The question for historians is why was the Helmsman's observance of the lookouts so important that Fleet would angrily swear vengeance against Hitchens to a reporter, in violation of a job threatening gag order while under guard?

Hitchens later testified under oath he couldn't see anything while behind the wheel but according to Fleet, that is not what he said in the States. With the 2010 granddaughter's revelations, we sense a scared Hitchens was looking to spread blame around. With his hands on the wheel, his only option was to point a finger at the respected but now dead First Officer. He worried he could be the fall guy for the whole disaster.

The point Fleet wanted to make, but could not let on about, was that Hitchens could not have seen Fleet speaking down the mast ladder to Lee during the *"up back"* conversation. Bent forward to shout into the tube, Fleet would have been concealed by the mast's girth.

But during their first meeting Hitchens could have said he looked forward at the bell sounding. He may have asked questions like, *"Where was Lee the whole time?"* He may have known Lee

Evidential Details

was gone and could have told Director Ismay about Lee's absence while the lookouts had hoped to keep that a secret.

Early on these men must have realized somebody could be hanged or spend the rest of their life in prison for what happened. Now engaged in a triangularization of argument it all comes full circle when you reflect on why Fleet was so frightened in the U.S. Disaster Hearings. He felt he was fighting for his life.

It is both understandable and unfortunate for historians that Fleet skipped over the time period just after he climbed down from the crow's nest.

Smith - "Did you go up to the bridge?
Fleet – "I went up on the boat deck.
Smith - "What did they say to you up there?
Fleet - "I did not see anyone there; I seen them all at the boats, getting ready and putting them out.
Smith - "The life boats?
Fleet: "Yes, sir.
Smith: "What did you do?
Fleet: "I helped to get the port boat out.

Evidential Details

Interview Clarification

Question: Generally speaking, how much...information should be given a viewer in operations / applications?

Joseph McMoneagle: None. Zero. What you can do if the target requires a response or a description of an individual, you can say, "*Describe the individual at* (whatever location)" and the location needs to be hidden (would be a number, for instance). If you were targeting let's say a church, and there was an individual in that church, the church would be coded as say, "location A1". It would then say, "*describe individual at location A1*".

Under no condition can you give any information that is directly pertinent to the target. There is never any front-loading. The reason for this is because the entire concept of remote viewing is that an individual is forced, has no choice, but to use their psi ability to answer the requirement. Any info that is given in any way, or form, modifies that response in a way that removes / reduces the probability of accuracy.

"The 'giggle factor' associated with remote viewing or psychic functioning continues to block earnest attempts at using these functions for humankind's benefit."

Joseph McMoneagle ~ *The Ultimate Time Machine*

Evidential Details

End Game

After the Last Lifeboat

Resilient man picks up his tools and his arts, and moves on, taking his memories with him. If education has deepened and broadened those memories, civilization migrates with him, and builds somewhere another home.

Will and Ariel Durant

Captain's Death

In 1898 the thirty-six year old American author named Morgan Robertson (1861-1915) published a premonition from what he referred to as his "astral writing partner." Fourteen years ahead of the Titanic disaster, his farfetched story entitled Futility, described a marine behemoth named the Titan. His was a tale of a ship so immense people in the nineteenth century waved the story off as sheer fiction. But ultimately, what made this narrative memorable was his detail about the still unbuilt *Titanic's* future disaster.

Robertson's psychic vision described a three propeller ship of British registry foundering in the Atlantic after striking an iceberg on the starboard side in month of April. With a top speed of 24-25 knots, his vessel carried approximately 3,000 passengers. The book also foretold of the inadequacy of the doomed liner's life boats. After the disaster skeptics maintained this was pure chance.

Nonetheless, the ship in his story had a 70,000 ton displacement which was only 5% unlike *Titanic*. The ship's length was only 9% different. The lifeboat count was only off by four. His tale foretold of marine architecture not yet designed. The *Titan* had nineteen watertight bulkheads below deck; the *Titanic* had fifteen. Prophesying the ship would not be at capacity, Robertson's passenger count was only 10% off the actual roster. Unfortunately he did not make known how the Captain died.

Captain Edward John Smith's death remains a mystery because nobody who saw him die lived. This meant there was no history and virtually any story could become accepted if repeated enough. Though referred to as an Edwardian Sea Captain he was age 51 when the Victorian Era came to a close in 1901. A career merchant mariner, he had prior maiden voyage captaining experience and was considered the best in the business. At age 62, *Titanic's* maiden voyage was to crown his career. It was his retirement cruise at the helm of the world's greatest luxury liner.

Discussion focuses on how Smith could preside over this disaster when *Titanic* had been in receipt of wireless ice warnings from numerous vessels including the Captain's old command *RMS Baltic*. The ship's bridge had even responded to a signal lamp warning at 10:30 p.m. from *S.S. Rappahannock* just an hour and ten minutes before impact.

Evidential Details

Even though the voyage was ahead of its scheduled five a.m. New York arrival, the ship was full speed ahead even as other Captains in the vicinity had come to a halt awaiting sunrise.[1] One reason for this was given in White Star's Managing Director J. Bruce Ismay's testimony before the U.S. Senate Hearings:

Ismay - *"The Titanic being a new ship, we were gradually working her up. When you bring out a new ship you naturally do not start running her at full speed until you get everything working smoothly and satisfactorily down below.*[i]

Information is not readily available on Edward Smith apart from his maritime career. He was born in January 27, 1850 at Hanley, Stoke-on-Trent, in the Staffordshire Potteries during British Prime Minister Palmerston's Administration. He left school at age 13, moved to Liverpool and became a seaman apprentice.[ii]

Smith started his career on the clipper ship *Senator Webber* in 1869. Competent, he rose through the ranks joining White Star Lines in 1880 as a fourth officer on a ship called the *Celtic*, whose command he would ultimately assume. In just seven years he became Captain of White Star's *Republic*.[iii] By the century's turn, he would command the larger *Baltic*.

During South Africa's Boer War (1899–1902) Smith commanded military support ships earning him the British Transport Medal, the Naval Reserves Decoration and the rank of Commander in the Royal Naval Reserve.[iv] He had efficiently ferried men and supplies into a South African military effort whose mid-campaign reorganization emerged as a major British setback.

In 1904, Smith became a Commodore and would, from then on command White Star's flagship. In 1911, he was selected to captain *Titanic's* sister ship *RMS Olympic*.

In 1912 he resided on Winn Road in the Southampton suburb of Westwood, Hampshire. By that April, he had been in command of seventeen ships and had 32 years with White Star Line. As the *Titanic* was tugged toward open water, Smith had over two million miles with White Star.[v] In space travel, this is equivalent

---

[1] Thirty-nine years earlier, White Star Line had claimed the North Atlantic record for the world's largest commercial marine disaster killing almost 550 people.

95

Captain's Death

to 8.5 round trips to the moon at approximately 20 miles per hour. As a man, "His personality radiated authority, tact, good humor, and confidence. He had a pleasant, quiet voice and a ready smile."[vi] He was also the highest paid Captain on the high seas.[2]

Illustrated London News
Titanic's Captain Edward John Smith with medals. (1850-1912)

---

[2] The Captain's salary of 1,250 Pounds Sterling has been alternatively represented as on a monthly basis and on a "p.a." basis (per annum). Compare Smith's compensation in today's terms. As the year 1912 opened the Dollar to Pounds Sterling conversion was $4.87. This compensated Smith US$ 6,086.62 per year not including his free room and board. By 1997, this would equal over $102,737 yearly. Compare this with the 240 Pounds Sterling per month (US$1,168) paid the Captain of the vessel *California* which is just over $19,715 in 1997 dollars. Captain Smith was also eligible for a yearly $1000 safety bonus. (*New York Times* "Money and Exchange" page, Cable and Sight Rates Section, Jan. 3, 1912.)

Evidential Details

McMoneagle – Smith after the impact – ...a man who is approximately five feet seven inches tall, and stocky. He appears to be about 170 - 180 pounds. His hair, beard and mustache are predominantly white with some silver and dark gray. At the time of the event, he is fully dressed in a white uniform with epaulets on his shoulders. What appears to be a double-breasted suit - - four buttons, and a white belt (which may be hiding two more buttons). White pants, white shirt with black bow-tie (not the modern version), but what looks like a loosely tied silk. He is not wearing a hat as he either lost it in the confusion or chose to leave it in the cabin.

Over the years, Captain Smith had developed qualities appealing to clientele able to afford luxurious Trans-Atlantic travel. "Many of the western world's richest and most celebrated people would often plan their trips specially just so they could sail with Smith and enjoy his genial personality and after dinner good humour, which never interfered with his air of authority and tact, even when chatting with children for whom he invariably had plenty of time."[vii] Much the equivalent of a successful battlefield general, Smith looked the part and spoke the British maritime vernacular of an authentic high seas Captain. His Officers thought him disciplinarian but fair. He instilled confidence in all and pressed on through hazardous seas to keep sailing schedules.

As a socialite, Smith's knowledge of marine operations and world ports of call fit nicely with the high society conversation circulating throughout the first class lounge. As a result, a dinner, "at the sixth table on the forward end of the saloon; back toward the bow of the ship,"[viii] was a much sought after invitation.

By 1912, *Titanic*'s operational circumstances had come to include various aspects of luxury hotel management with passenger relations constantly in motion. With the world's first fresh water thirty-two foot below deck swimming pool to provision, the Captain also kept an eye on the subcontractors. This included the French speaking al la carte restaurateur; the nine roaming ship construction contract guarantors; the Royal Post Office staff; and the Marconi International Communications Company wireless employees situated behind the wheel house, and the ship's eight

Captain's Death

musicians from a Liverpool Agency.[3]

Since history ends with what the last survivor recounts, we reviewed all the stories describing Captain Smith's final sightings. What emerged were half a dozen tales about his death. What is known is that evening Captain Smith had dinner with the Widners and Mr. and Mrs. Thayer. Afterwards Mrs. Widener stated:

"On the night of Sunday, the 14th of April, 1912, my husband and I gave a dinner at which Captain Smith was present. Captain Smith drank absolutely no wine or intoxicating liquor of any kind whatever at the dinner."[ix]

Colonel Archie Butt, U.S. President William Harding Taft's special envoy, may have also stopped by the table. After dinner Smith checked in on the bridge at 8:55 p.m. with Second Officer Charles Lightoller.

They discussed ice reports, the extreme calmness of the sea, and at what point the ship would be in the ice field's vicinity. They agreed the lookouts should be able to spot ice-bergs approximately four miles out; plenty of time to alter course. Concerned, Smith left the helm and retired to his quarters about 9:20 p.m. requesting to be contacted immediately should conditions appear, "*at all doubtful*". Forty minutes later the Officers shift changed.[4]

After the impact, witnesses agree Smith re-emerged from his cabin within one minute. After hearing what happened he ordered a carpenter to take a sounding and asked Fourth Officer Joseph Groves Boxhall, 28, to inspect below deck and report on the extent of the damage.[5]

McMoneagle - The Captain has both his Number One

---

[3] The musicians were represented by the Amalgamated Musicians Union and were employed by the Black Agency in Liverpool. Before the voyage, their wages had been reduced to 4 Pounds Sterling and their uniform allowance eliminated. None survived. After the disaster, Black Agency presented the bereaved families with a bill of 14 shillings, 7 pence (USD16.20) each for the uniforms that were not returned as per their contractual obligations.

[4] In sea worthiness trials, the *Titanic* had performed well in circling tests. This may have influenced the Captains thinking about the ship's maneuverability that night.

[5] Officer Boxhall would be the last *Titanic* Officer to die in England at age 83; in April, 1967, 55 years later to the month.

Evidential Details

(First Officer Murdock) **as well as his Chief Engineer** (Joseph Bell) **with him in the Wheel House. There are four other officers there as well, but they appear to be coming and going - - probably carrying orders to areas of the ship, which he can't communicate directly. I have a sense that in this immediate confusion the Captain had his crew passing instructions to the passengers, which actually had a calming effect. I see the Captain on the First Class and Second Class decks in this first twenty minutes of striking the iceberg. My sense is that he is totally in control of both his men and himself. A clear sense of duty is evident.**

Just after midnight the damage report came back. The conclusion was that mathematically the ship must founder. Smith also knew the ship's lifeboat count and realized many would perish unless help arrived. He went to the wireless room. "A few moments later the *Titanic* became the first ever passenger ship to send out an SOS."[x]

McMoneagle - He has also ordered two men - young men, probably 22 - 25 years of age, to man the short-wave as well as the long wave transmitters in the communications center, to try and raise help... They are both transmitting in International Morse Code - - the name of the ship, followed by a series of three SOS's - - then repeated. My sense is they manned these stations throughout the event...

Titanic had the most modern communication equipment available in 1912. This included a multiple channel tuner as well as the ship's Magnetic Detector. The 1.5-kilowatt transmitters had a 400 mile range during the day and at least 1,000 miles at night.

McMoneagle – Captain's death preparations - The specific event appears to have actually begun at about 12 - 14 minutes past Midnight. The Captain was not in his quarters, but was on the First Class Deck in the lounge area when the event began. I see that is where he left his hat. He is sitting at a large table which seats approximately 12 people, but there are only five other gentlemen there with him ...none are crew, all are passengers. They are drinking what appears to be Port or some other dark red wine in crystal glasses and smoking

Captain's Death

cigars. Although, I don't see the Captain smoking - - he may not smoke cigars. My sense is that he is a pipe smoker and prefers to enjoy his pipe only in his quarters.

It was at this point the First Class passengers were informed. Total sinking time would be approximately 2 hours and 40 minutes.

McMoneagle - The Captain has returned to the Wheel House. He is assuming command of his ship in the place that he knows he can control it from. He has requested information from the ship's engineers as to the extent of the damage and he knows it is serious. At this time he has ordered preparation be made to abandon ship and launch the lifeboats.

By approximately 12:35 a.m. the ship is beginning to list heavily forward. My sense is the deck is now at about a 12-degree angle, from front to rear. The Captain is attempting to use pumps in non-damaged areas with line carried through to the forward areas, to help at least slow the descent. There is something wrong with the compartment doors (seals)... Either the assigned crew hasn't closed them, or the ship's hull has warped just enough that they will no longer seal. While the Captain can't know it, there are more than five compartments that are flooding. Even worse, I see cross flooding between the dual hulls of the ship. Observationally, it appears there are five compartments flooding, however, I see water moving through the double-hull sections into a sixth and seventh compartment. Likewise, there is a shift of water from the compartments, which is beginning to take place three decks above the bilge area. Again, I have a sense that sealdoors either were not closed off, or were opened for some reason.

This confirms bulkhead doors played a role in the sinking. They may have been bent by the impact. The water going back seven compartments between the double hulls confirms the results of *Titanic* being ordered to continue forward for about ten minutes.

McMoneagle - The Captain has ordered all women be placed in the lifeboats. It appears to now be about 12:45 a.m. There is confusion in families because this essentially means

Evidential Details

they will be splitting men off from wives and children, however, I do not get a sense of panic taking place here. It is more business-like than that. It is almost as if everyone is just accepting this as a matter of course.[6] The only crew allowed to leave the ship are the crewmen responsible for each of the lifeboats. These are pre-assigned stations and...the ship's officers are not getting onto these lifeboats.[7]

I sense a lot of confusion among the ship's crew. There are many efforts to try and save the ship, but in their hearts, they know the cause is lost. The Captain essentially supports these efforts until about 1:05 a.m. Most of the lifeboats are now away and the few remaining are loading men and some of the crew. There is no drawing of lots here, so I get a sense the older gentlemen are deciding among themselves who should go and who shouldn't. They are attempting to load those men with families first, followed by younger crew-members who won't be of benefit to keeping the boat afloat. I also get a strong sense there are still many women onboard who have chosen to stay with their husbands. I sense everyone feels help will arrive in time to pluck them from the ship before it sinks. This... (is) a false hope generated by the slow flooding taking place below decks. The ship is hopelessly lost but the water is invading other decks so slowly that no one knows this. The deck is now listing approximately 20 degrees.

Lookout Fred Fleet departed from the Port side in lifeboat #6 with Quartermaster Hitchens. Reginald Robinson Lee's boat #13 did not shove off from the Starboard side until about 1:35 a.m.

McMoneagle - They rowed some distance from the ship, approximately 1 - 1.5 miles, where the boats were collected together as best they could be. I don't believe they were lashed together, but they were kept together by the men with the oars.

---

[6] "It was perfect order. The discipline was splendid. The officers were carrying out their duty and I think the passengers behaved splendidly. I did not see a cowardly act by any man." Major Peuchen's testimony - U.S. Senate Disaster Hearings.

[7] Early on this was true. By the end Third Officer Pitman, Fourth Officer Boxhall, and Fifth Officer Lowe did lead lifeboats away from the ship.

Captain's Death

The oars helped the boats move alongside each other and passengers were shifted to equalize the occupancy count. The lifeboats were not 'lashed' together but they did have little ropes called "Painters" attached to the boat's bow for mooring. At about dawn a ship named *Carpathia* arrived. It had traveled 58 miles to the rescue at full speed.

* * *

Titanic's wireless technology played an important part in the effort to save the passengers. In *The Maiden Voyage,* author Geoffrey Marcus comments on the popular acclaim the inventor received. "It was probably the proudest moment of Marconi's career. The highest tributes were showered upon him from all parts of the world. The value and importance of the marvelous new invention had been demonstrated in a manner beyond all possible doubt."[xi] And in that day, anyone operating this high technology commanded prestige.

The last message transmitted by *Titanic* radiomen was, "*Come quick; our engine room is filling up to the boilers.*"[xii] It would be radioman Harold Sydney Bride's testimony that was largely accepted as the "eye-witness" account to Captain Smith's death.

But even before the *Titanic's* rescue ship *Carpathia* got to New York, a controversy developed concerning Harold Bride's refusal to send a survivors list until money could be paid. In what became early 20th Century checkbook journalism the wireless operator withheld information until he was awarded big money for an interview that appeared on the front page of the United States largest newspaper - the *New York Times.*

What emerged was a public right to know outrage set against an Englishman leveraging payouts from a foreign (American) press establishment. The upshot was that the U.S. Senate went to the top of the Marconi Wireless Company for clarification. A Summons was issued to thirty-four year old Nobel Prize winner Gugliemo Marconi, the inventor of amplified wireless radio.

First off, Senator Smith entered the communications between the Marconi Company Office and wireless operator Harold Bride into the Congressional Record. As the *Carpathia* was still

Evidential Details

enroute to New York, Marconi Office telegrams to Bride said:

8:12 p.m. *"Say, old man Marconi Co. taking care of you. Keep your mouth shut, and hold your story. It is fixed for you to get big money."*

8:30 p.m. *"Arranged for your exclusive story for dollars in four figures, Mr. Marconi agreeing. Say nothing until you see me."* (Signed) J.M. Sammis Opr. C.

The Senate was appalled and Mr. Marconi[8] was then forced to re-take the stand before the Disaster subcommittee.
Senator Smith - (disgusted) "...let me ask you this. With the right to exact compensation for an exclusive story detailing the horrors of the greatest sea disaster that ever occurred in the history of the world, do you mean that an operator under your company's direction shall have the right to prevent the public from knowing of that calamity --
Marconi - "No.
- "except through the exclusive appropriation of the facts by the operator who is cognizant of them?
Marconi - "I say, not at all."[xiii]

On the defensive, one of the twentieth century's great inventors denied he had authorized any suppression of information. But the Committee was not convinced. So on Monday April 29, 1912, the ninth day of the Hearings, Frederick M. Sammis, 35, General Engineer of the Marconi Wireless Telegraph Co. of America took the stand. How much money Harold Bride received for his story was of great interest. Referring to the *Titanic* and the *Carpathia* wireless operators, Sammis was asked:
Senator Smith - "Did they receive their money?
Sammis - "I understand they did, and more besides.
Smith - "How much more?
Sammis - "I understand they got $250 (US$6,567/2018) more

---

[8] Guglielmo Marchese Marconi (1874-1937) is the Italian physicist credited as having developed wireless telegraphy. In 1909, he shared the Nobel Prize in Physics with Karl Braun. Ironically, he and his family were to have been on *Titanic* that spring, but they sailed earlier on the Cunard Lines *Lusitania*. One month before the disaster, Marconi had been awarded an enormous contract to wire communications throughout the British Empire. He wanted the United States account.

apiece than was promised them.
Smith - "That is they got $750 (US$19,702/2018) a piece?
Sammis - "That is my rough recollection: I did not see the money or handle it, and do not wish to. That is hearsay. (Bride testified he received $1,000 [US$26,270/2018] and *Carpathia's* operator Harold Thomas Cottam received $750.)
Smith - "Were these payments made through yourself or any other officer of the Marconi Company?
Sammis - "I have already stated that I did not see the money, did not expect to, and did not wish to.
Smith - "Let us clear this up as we go along. I think it is a most distasteful matter to you, as it is to the committee, and I think to the public.
Sammis - "I have not done anything I am ashamed of, and if I can clear my record, that the newspapers have impugned, I want to do it, and I am sure you want to help me.[xiv]

But the day before radioman Harold Bride was to appear before the U.S. Senate, a press interview from *Carpathia's* wireless room appeared on the front page of the April 19, 1912 *New York Times*.[xv] And as expected, the discussion started with questions about Bride's withholding information. So it is not surprising of the 244 published sentences, the first words out of his mouth were:
Harold Bride - "In the first place, the public should not blame anyone because more wireless messages about the disaster to the *Titanic* did not reach shore from *Carpathia*. I <u>positively refused</u> to send press dispatches because the bulk of personal messages with touching words of grief was so large.

"*Positively refused*". But whose decision was this to make and was this without financial motive? Bride was one of two operators that could control a news monopoly. The result was that individuals got paid private messages out rather than a general broadcast survivors list for the public's benefit. What irked the Senators was Bride's indifference toward an information blackout which included President Taft's inquiry about envoy Colonel Butt.

It was against this big money - big story - celebrity backdrop that Englishman Harold Bride (1890 - 1956) made his Senate appearance. "Bride transfixed those present, first with his dramatic

Evidential Details

New York Times

Harold Bride's name and story were front page (white arrows middle left) just below the headlines in the *New York Times* that quoted he had, *"Finished a stoker."*

Captain's Death

entrance in a wheelchair, his left foot in a bandage, and then with his account, one of the most astonishing sea stories ever told. It was at once a primer on the still unfamiliar world of wireless communications at sea, a tale of human obstinacy, and a firsthand chronicle of disaster foretold and dramatically realized."[xvi]

But in the Hearings Harold Bride was rude on a range of issues as evidenced by his attitude toward the other ship's wireless operators whom could have brought assistance to *Titanic*.

Bride - "The wireless operators aboard the (merchant vessel) *Chester* got all they asked for. And they were wretched operators. They knew American Morse but not Continental Morse sufficiently to be worthwhile. They taxed our endurance to the limit. I had to cut them out at last, they were insufferably slow... The *Chester's* man thought he knew it, but he was as slow as Christmas coming."

Returning later to ram this point home to the Committee:

Bride - "If the *Chester* had had a decent operator I could have worked with him longer but he got on my nerves with his insufferable incompetence."

Licensed on June 29, 1911, less than ten months earlier, the 22-year-old was no more charitable with United States Navy. The Naval vessels *USS North Dakota* and *Delaware* were in the area. Bride may have been in touch with both ships as he refers to the plural "Navy operators."

Bride - "The Navy operators were a great nuisance. I advised them all to learn the Continental Morse and learn to speed up in it if they ever expected to be worth their salt."

The Americans were inexperienced with "Continental Morse." But Morse code was developed by American Samuel F.B. Morse (1791-1872), not in Europe. Continental code differed from American Morse in eleven letters, its punctuation, and in all the numbers except the numeral four. The need for the Europeans to have made these changes was claimed to be speed but the differences were enough to slow communications. Bride knew of these differences and his chiding remarks illustrate his attitude toward Americans who were becoming very competitive in the North Atlantic maritime trade. Plus it covered the fact Bride did not know standard Morse. After these *Titanic* sessions this testimony was

Evidential Details

sent to McMoneagle.

Henry Aldridge & Son

This was to be wireless operator John "Jack" Phillip's (left) 25th birthday picture. But Harold Bride stood in his way and the senior wireless operator's eyes betray what he thought. Phillips did not survive leaving Bride free to testify to whatever suited the moment.

Captain's Death

McMoneagle - I will say, being a Morse operator myself, Bride is one arrogant ****er. The differences between Continental and American Morse are a handful of "cut numbers" and special symbols - which any Morse operator, who is a professional, will pick up and be able to deal with in a matter of a couple of hours. So, what he has to say about the other operators is nothing but BS and arrogance.

Mr. Bride's attitude is further revealed in the story about the Captain going to the wireless room to confirm the correct distress message was being sent. In what should have been a deadly serious moment he recalled:

Bride - "The humor of the situation appealed to me. I cut in with a little remark that made us all laugh, including the Captain. *Send S.O.S.* I said. *It's the new call, and it may be your last chance to send it.*"

Philadelphia Inquirer

Reviewing the photographs we were not surprised to find a grim faced Marconi (left) as Harold Bride testified under oath in the U.S. Senate Disaster Hearings.

This "humor" was in the face of a Captain who understood that he, the ship and over 1,500 people were doomed. So we wondered when Bride claimed it was senior operator Jack Phillips who sent the infamous message to the merchant vessel *Frankfurt* that their wireless operator "*was a fool.*"

Evidential Details

Testimony then uncovered that *Titanic's* wireless room had also ordered a potential rescue ship wireless key to "*shut up.*" Stunned at the callous disregard in the face of the world's largest maritime disaster Senator Smith explored:

Smith - "But in such an emergency do you not think that a more detailed statement might have been sent? Take, for instance, the message from the *Titanic* to the *Carpathia* that the boiler rooms were filling with water and the ship sinking; that could have been sent with perfect propriety to a boat that was in proximity, could it not?

Bride - "No sir; I do not think it could have been under the circumstances

This proved Bride lied under oath as Titanic was contacting ships in the area for approximately ninety minutes. The vessel *Frankfurt* had taken twenty minutes to respond, but a radio room time line analysis reveals there was ample opportunity for one of the two wireless men to follow up. Bride's willingness to ignore bonafide rescue alternatives astounded the Senators.

Smith - "Do you mean to say that the regulations under which you operate are such that in a situation of this character you have such discretionary power that you may dismiss an inquiry of that character --

Bride - (Interrupting) - "YOU USE YOUR COMMON SENSE.

Smith – without further word?

Bride - (In contempt) "You use your common sense, and the man on the *Frankfurt* apparently was not using his at the time.

Bride also proudly recounted to the *Times* his efforts to kill "*a stoker, or somebody from below decks*" who was attempting to take wireless operator Phillips' life jacket. Bride bludgeoned the Englishman in the back of the head. In a statement that could have remained forever secret he provided an opportunity for historians, and the upcoming British Inquiry, to observe his character.

Bride - "I suddenly felt a passion not to let that man die a decent sailor's death. I wished he might have stretched rope (been hanged) or walked the plank. I did my duty (lethal attack). I hope I finished him. I don't know. We left him on the cabin floor of the wireless room and he was not moving." Bride had now stated, for

Captain's Death

the record, he wished a *Titanic* crewman could walk the plank.

Philadelphia Inquirer

Harold Bride slouches down, lips pursed (center right) and head slightly tilted away from Corporate President Marconi's scornful look (far left). Marconi had seen the Senators faces. The last thing he needed was for an employee to make legislative enemies as he attempted to bring his business into the Unites States.

But in the British Hearings it was no surprise all this cruel and unusual, "*I hope I finished him*", bragging stopped. And all of a sudden it was Jack Philips who put the stoker down!

British Question 16775 – "Do I understand you to state that you thought it was a stoker who was taking this lifebelt off Mr. Phillips?

Bride – "I presumed from the appearance of the man that he was someone in that line of business.

16778 - "Do I understand that you hit him, or what?

Bride – "Well, we stopped him from taking the lifebelt off.

16779 - "We," you say?

Bride – "Yes.

16780 - "I understood the (Senate) report was that Mr. Phillips was engaged at this time with his work?

Bride – "Yes.

16781 - "Sending messages; and that you forced this man away?

Evidential Details

Bride – "Well, I forced the man away and it attracted Mr. Phillips's attention, and he came and assisted me.
16782 - "Is your recollection of this matter very clear?"
Bride – "It is fairly clear.
16784 - "You are supposed to have hit him?"
Bride – "Well, I held him and Mr. Phillips hit him.
16785 - "Mr. Phillips hit him?
Bride – "Yes.
16786 - "That is the difference between what you say and what I read. You are absolutely positive on this question?
Bride – "I am positive on it, yes.

Poor Phillips - more perjury against his memory. Bride had either killed or knocked an Englishman unconscious as the last collapsible lifeboat was loading. Nonetheless, as the lone radio room survivor, Harold Bride cashed in on the public's fascination about this most powerful wireless, on the world's greatest ship, caught up in the world's foremost tragedy.

But in Congress, it was different. The legislators realized there would be future incentives for wireless operators to withhold news or embellish information. This was such a concern it was taken up in the subcommittee's final report to the U.S. Senate.

"The disposition of officials of the Marconi Co. to permit this practice and the fact that company's representatives making the arrangements for the sale of the experiences of the operators of the Titanic and Carpathia subjects the participants to criticism, and the practice should be prohibited."[xvii]

As it turned out Harold Bride's real contribution to history was the American Radio Act of December, 1912 requiring all U.S. wireless operators to be licensed. In the future anyone imitating Bride's conduct faced immediate permit revocation. The bureau created to enforce these laws went on to become the American Federal Communications Commission in 1934.

So, with remote viewing sessions in hand, it was not surprising Bride waffled during his Captain's death testimony.
Senator Smith - "When did you last see the Captain? When he told you to take care of yourself?
Bride - "The last I saw of the Captain he went overboard from the

Captain's Death

Bridge, sir.
Smith - "What do you mean by overboard?
Bride - "He jumped overboard from the bridge. He jumped overboard from the bridge when we were launching the collapsible lifeboat.

So in the States, Captain Smith jumped overboard from the bridge. But what was unusual was that none of the numerous collapsible lifeboat survivors saw this. Again, a troubled Senator Smith attempted to resolve Bride's statements concerning the possibility the Captain might have jumped ship prematurely.
Smith - "The Captain at no time went over until the vessel sank?
Bride - "No sir.
Smith - "He went with the vessel?
Bride - "Practically speaking, yes sir.[xviii]

This line of inquiring was continued in Washington D.C.
Smith - "I want you to tell again, because there seems to be a little confusion about it, when you last saw the captain of the *Titanic*.
Bride - "The last I saw of the captain of the *Titanic*, he went overboard from the bridge about, I should think, <u>three minutes</u> before I left it myself.
Smith - "Did he have a life preserver on?
Bride - "I could not say, sir.

So, did the Captain go overboard as the bridge settled below the water line, or did he go over when the radiomen left some 20 minutes later? With this time line discrepancy, and a trans-Atlantic voyage to think it over, it was no surprise Bride's story changed. Now, to minimize cross-examination in the British Hearings, he submitted his revised story in writing.
Bride - "Here is a paper, sir that may be of interest to you. It is a report which I have made to Mr. Cross, the traffic manager of the Marconi Co.:

"*I now assisted in pushing off a collapsible lifeboat, which was on the port side of the forward funnel, onto the boat deck. Just as the boat fell I noticed Capt. Smith dive from the bridge into the sea.*"[xix]

So in the States Bride swore Captain Smith had jumped – presumably feet first. But in England Bride put in writing the Cap-

Evidential Details

tain dove – presumably head first. And he (insincerely) could not tell if the Captain was wearing one of *Titanic's* large new beige life jackets over his uniform with deck lights fully lit! Nonetheless, some *Titanic* historians insists dodgy character, multiple perjuries, economic incentive, possible diminished celebrity, along with his aggravated battery bravado are only circumstantial reasons to doubt his steadfast commitment to the truth about the *Titanic's* most quoted Captain's death scenario.

Daily Sketch

Back in England with his father Arthur, sporting a dapper new look from his American press proceeds, Harold Bride first testified under oath he saw Captain Smith jump, but later in England dive from the bridge. For the next 100 years this twenty-two year-old had history's final word on this major detail of *Titanic's* most responsible individual.

Like other key people in the *Titanic* saga Harold Bride became elusive. After the disaster hearings, he moved on as a telegrapher for the Post Office. Later he was aboard HMS *Mona's Isle* and SS *Medina*. Then he left the wireless business altogether and moved to Scotland winding up as a pharmacy salesman. He married Lucy Downie and moved to Stepps, Lanarkshire, under the alias of MacBride where they raised three children.

Captain's Death

Surfacing in 1954, in what was a critical blow to his veracity, Bride gave an interview to Ernest Robinson regarding the reported suicide of First Officer Murdoch. Now Bride contradicted himself about his whereabouts that night. He reassured a hometown audience claiming he was with First Officer Murdoch when he died and that he had not committed suicide.

Bride was aware people still accepted his Captain Smith story so 42 years later he finally told the world he had witnessed the First Officer's death as well. But not surprisingly, no one ever reported Bride as being on that side of the ship. Nor did he have the time. Bride and Phillips worked continuously until Captain Smith's last minute release well after Officer Murdoch had fallen overboard from a gunshot wound to the head. And when departing, Bride was fixed upon getting into the last collapsible lifeboat.

Harold Bride died of lung cancer on Sunday April 29, 1956 in a Glasgow, Scotland hospital at age 66 and was cremated on May 2. Without remote viewing, his Captain going over from the bridge stories – jumped or dove - would have lived on for eternity.

The actual timeline shows that had the Captain remained on the bridge he would have been forced off as it slowly settled into the water before his last wireless room visit. Moreover, Bride's story is disputed by the historically overlooked testimony of an unpaid, hence unconflicted, eyewitness Henry Samuel Etches, 41, a Bedroom Steward from Southampton, England.

Observing the bridge as his lifeboat number five departed, from the vessel's front, Mr. Etches gave eyewitness testimony concerning the moments the *Titanic's* bridge started under.

Senator Smith - "Could you see the bridge when the ship went down?
Etches - "You could see it quite plain, sir.
Smith - "Did you see anybody on the bridge?
Etches - "Not a soul, sir.[xx]

Later Etches testified that if the Captain had been inside the wheelhouse he might not have seen him but this was still not jumping or diving off the bridge. Mr. Etches was also in a position to see Captain Smith swimming around as *Titanic's* lights were still operating at full brightness.

Evidential Details

Washington Evening Star
Members of the *Titanic* crew in New York. Bedroom Steward Henry Etches (far back right) with Frederick Fleet (second from left), lookout George Hogg (fourth from right back row) and Archie Jewel (fourth from left).

Captain's Death

Even Bride fails to mention the Captain who, according to his testimony, should have been in front of him in the water.

Bride - "There were men all around me – hundreds of them. The sea was dotted with them, all depending on their lifeboats. I felt I simply had to get away from the ship. She was a beautiful sight then."[xxi]

Mr. Etches testimony has generally been ignored because saying what did not happen provided no alternative scenario. But Bride's account was one of heroism – a great Captain standing on the bridge as the massive ship went down. This version is well summed up by author Geoffrey Marcus. In *The Maiden Voyage* he gives us one version of Captain Smith at the end:

"It was about this time that Captain Smith again appeared in the wireless cabin. He said, '*Men, you have done your full duty you can do no more. Abandon your cabin. Now it's every man for himself. Look out for yourselves. I release you. That's the way of it at this kind of a time. Every man for himself!*' After this the Captain returned to the Boat Deck remarking to a man here and there as he passed, '*It's every man for himself*.'"[xxii]

A bridge story witness, First Class Steward Frederick Ray, said he saw the Captain back on the bridge with his personal steward. But when was unclear, and the Captain may well have visited the bridge one last time before it settled underwater. Smith is also said to have been in the navigation room getting final bearings.

Another death scenario is offered in *Her Name Titanic*. Author Charles Pellegrino writes the Captain's final order was "*Be British, Boys. Be British.*" The narrative continues: "...Harold Bride saw him dive into the water just before the bridge vanished. Someone else saw him swimming out there, trying to aid a child. No one ever saw him again."[xxiii]

In a picture displayed in the book *Titanic – The Truth Behind the Disaster*, an artist depicts Smith, no baby, as he, "*swims towards an upturned collapsible*"[xxiv] lifeboat, his Captains hat still in place.

Captain Smith was rightfully respected. So much so that Bride's legend about the Captain going down on the bridge would actually take on a life of its own. Fireman Harry Senior would go on

Evidential Details

Illustrated London News

A depiction of a courageous act with artistic license. The Captain was nowhere near the overturned lifeboats, the nightscape was star light, the Captain's uniform was white, no babies were rescued from a collapsible lifeboat, and no one claimed a baby rescued by the Captain was buried at sea.

Captain's Death

to report he saw the Captain bring a baby to a lifeboat. Then, Steward J. Maynard reportedly claimed he actually received an infant delivered up from the water by the Captain himself. So what happened to this baby? The moviemakers of *Titanic* (1997) portrayed the Captain dying in the wheelhouse even though saving a baby would have been a nice little side story.

No one would deny there were infants that went into the water. But a baby could not have survived that freezing exposure to be delivered up alive. Nor was an infant's corpse buried at sea from any lifeboat that night.

More to the point, author Michael Davie states the Captain died five different deaths. Some of the versions are that Smith shot himself, jumped over the side of the ship or went down in his quarters. There has also been speculation the Captain was killed swimming when the first steam funnel fell forward! Until now no one really knew, so many simply quoted Bride's story.

It would not be until 1997 that author Paul Quinn broached the subject in *Titanic at Two A.M.*: "Where was Captain Smith? Lightoller does not mention him being present at this time on the port side, and nobody makes mention of him on the starboard side either. It is a gallant thought to imagine him "*on the bridge to the last*", but realistically, there was nothing there to be done..."[xxv]

Titanic was descending into the water starboard bow first as the front five of its sixteen compartment rivets had been ripped below the water line. Once he was fully informed, Captain Smith realized his death was certain. Clearly, the bridge would be underwater before the ship sank. He had approximately 145 minutes left. What were his options?

After the last lifeboat should he face the peril of the gradually encroaching 28 degree (-2 C) saltwater and die a slow muscle paralysis death due to frigid exposure? He had a gun. Should he shoot himself? Or should he retreat aft to join an increasingly terrorized mob of employees and passengers?

Through remote viewing we found it came down to what the Captain knew about ship's stores. What follows is another *Titanic* disclosure about the Captain's humanitarian actions on behalf of his passengers. And what is so salient about his absence

Evidential Details

from the bridge is his common sense approach to events.

McMoneagle - **After the last lifeboat is away the Captain has ordered all remaining passengers to the aft salon of the First Class deck. My sense is this is a smaller salon than the others as it has no fancy glass ceiling or large and wide expanse. My sense is there are many chairs and lounges here and it is some sort of reading or lounging area. It may in fact be a gaming room or something like that.**[9]

Harlan & Wolfe

Though the actual list was toward the camera, the First Class Smoking Room is shown here at a 22 degree tilt. By the time the ship broke in two the list had doubled. With the eerie metallic bending, creaking, and structural cracking sounds historian can imagine the fright on the passengers faces as the Captain addressed them on how to die. He stood in front of the table and chairs shown here.

The deck is listing 22 degrees forward and it is becoming difficult to stand or walk. The Captain has ordered the bar open and is sitting at a large table, which faces toward the bow of the boat. It is located approximately two thirds back

---

[9] The last life boat number four was lowered from the starboard side at 1:55 a.m. carrying Director J. Bruce Ismay.

Captain's Death

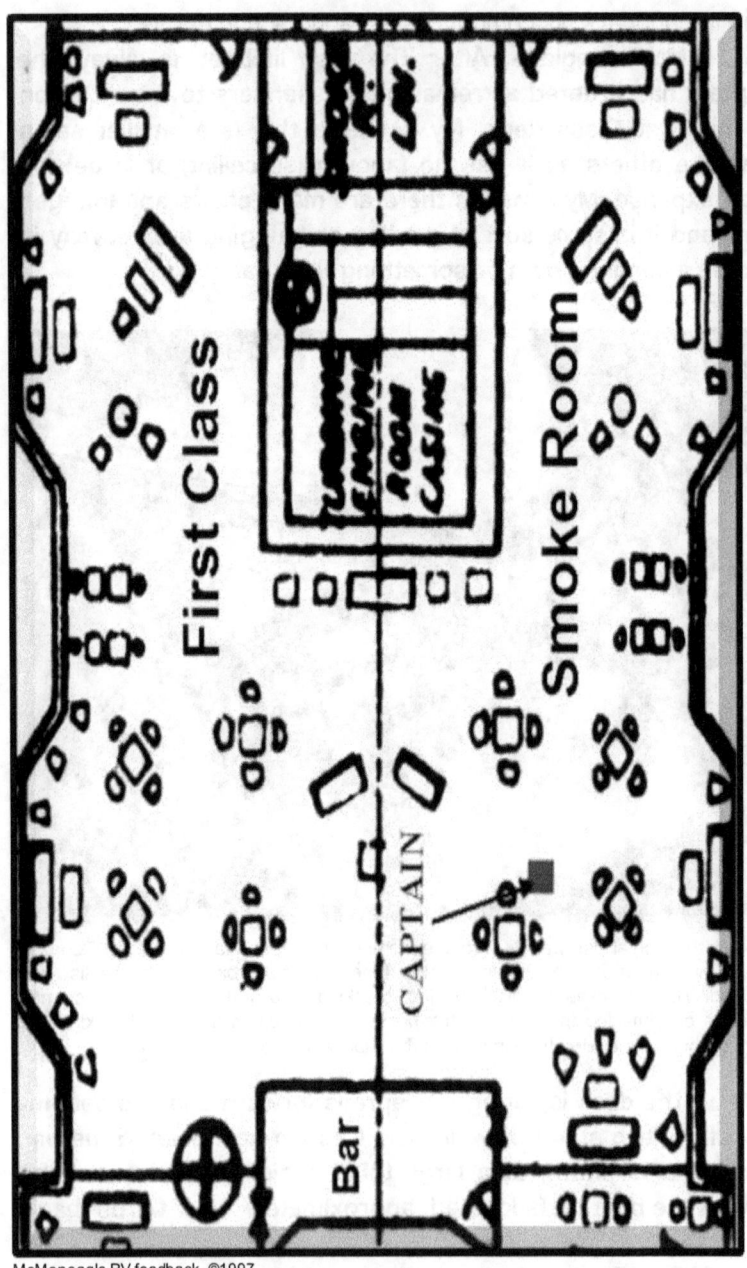

McMoneagle RV feedback - ©1997

McMoneagle – *Attached is where the Captain was standing - most of the time anyway* (left center). This is where the bow tore apart from the stern.

Evidential Details

from the forward wall of the lounge area. I feel a great sense of loss in him. He is visibly shaken by what has happened, but doing his best to present a tough exterior to the remaining passengers who have crowded into the lounge area.

Fireman "Paddy" Dillon - "Men in evening clothes were still playing cards on grotesquely slanting tables. Liquor was now "on the house" and available to all classes."[xxvi]

McMoneagle – The Captain - He has a large container, which looks like a footlocker or steamer trunk on the floor to his right side. The footlocker/steamer-trunk is a light gray color with a band of white approximately eighteen inches wide that runs around it width - wise (about the middle). There is a red cross which is about eight by eight inches in the center of the top.

My sense is that it has been brought from the medical station where numerous bottles and packages were hastily thrown into it. The Captain is explaining that there are powerful drugs in this trunk, which he is willing to pass out among the passengers. He isn't sure which drugs will cause an overdose, but he has an older woman (Catherine Wallis) **standing beside him that knows which drugs are which.**

In our follow-up, McMoneagle said he did not think the lady worked in the infirmary but was stationed in some kind of health spa area which could have been the pool or the Turkish Baths.[10] After having explained the medicines, she probably returned below deck to her room as McMoneagle could not recall that she stayed in the Smoking Lounge.

McMoneagle - Most of the drugs in the trunk are liquid. I have a sense the primary narcotic content of these liquids is

---

[10] It was uncanny how McMoneagle's Turkish Baths reference brought everything into context on F Deck. As Head Matron, 20 people reported to Catherine Wallis. She was familiar with the health remedies, which was why the Captain had her explain the medicine to the passengers. She also oversaw the large laundry and pressing rooms. On the same deck was the squash racquet court, the swimming bath, the showers, the Turkish baths, the hot room, steam room, shampoo room, the dry room and dressing rooms. Mrs. Wallis was also responsible for the 198,900-piece ships inventory of sheets, towels, eiderdown quilts and all the other miscellaneous items known as linens.

Captain's Death

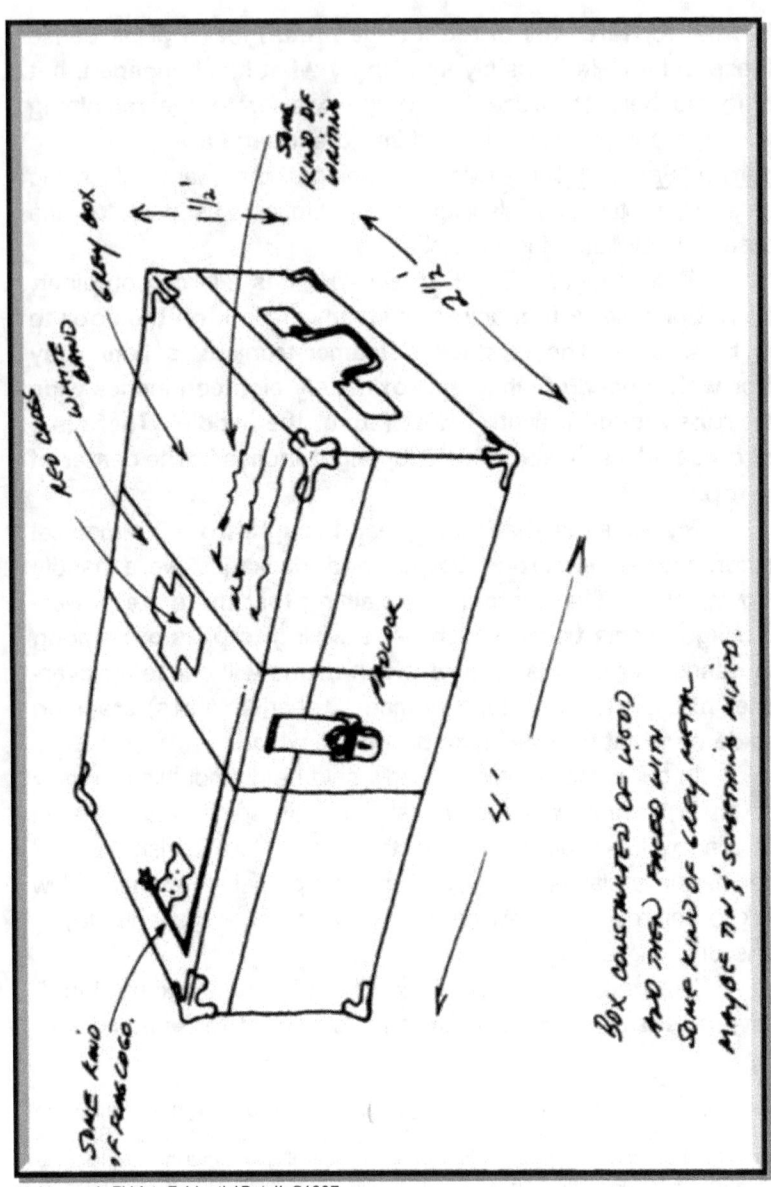

McMoneagle RV Art - Evidential Details ©1997

McMoneagle's dimensionalized Sea Trunk (122 x 67 x 38 cm) that Mrs. Wallis used to bring the medicine up to the First Class Smoking Lounge. Lower left on the trunk says "*some kind of flag logo*" shows cognition for the White Star Line 5 point star. The writing (lower left) says, "*Box constructed of wood and then faced with some kind of grey metal; maybe tin & something mixed.*"

Evidential Details

Inside the Trunk

Sketch C: reads left - right:

Six to a paper box packaged in cotton swabbing top & bottom.

The Morphine Kit

All glass ampoule. Long thin neck. Liquid inside is gold or amber in color.

Heavy metal syringe

The proper size glass syringe insert was displayed at a 2011 *Titanic* Exposition in the States.

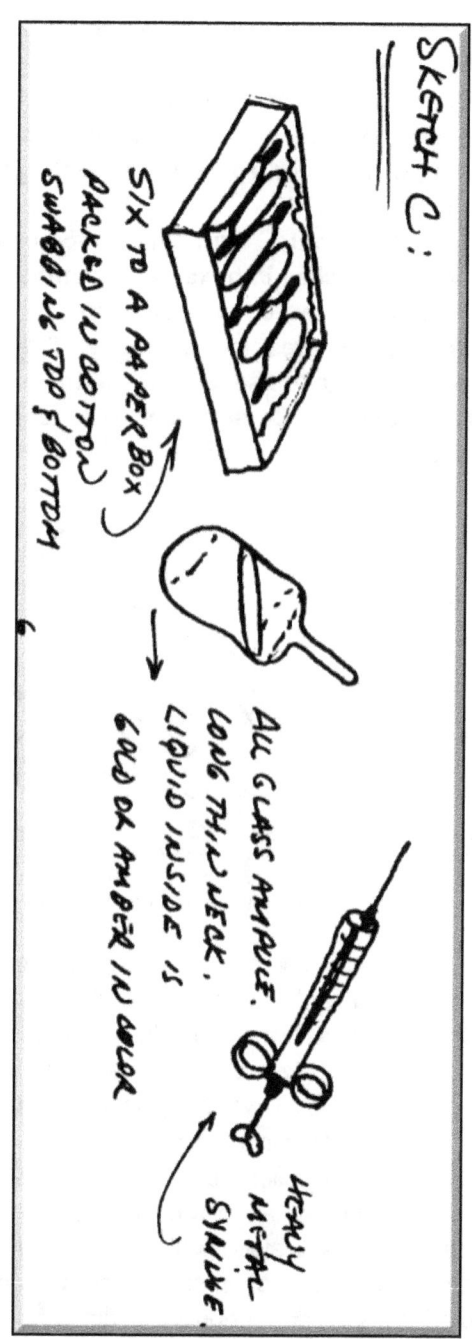

McMoneagle RV Art
Evidential Details ©1997

codeine in various degrees. Most of the liquid is for use either as a painkiller or for severe colds. There are two types of bottles. There are not enough of the bottles to go around. There are also bottles of laudanum, the content of which are full strength, intended to be mixed with other ingredients by the physician.

There are morphine ampoules (small glass vials) which are packed in boxes with cotton. These are passed out with syringes, which are made from metal and are much larger than the syringes in use today. The Captain is telling the passengers that use of any of these drugs in combination with alcohol will be sufficient to at least put them into a deep sleep.

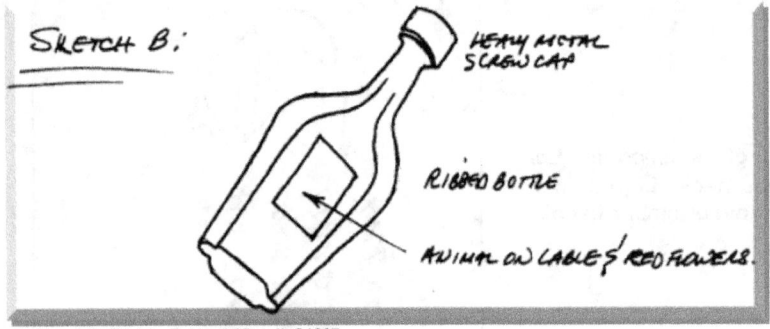

McMoneagle RV Art – Evidential Details©1997
The description reads: "**Heavy metal screw cap; Ribbed bottle; Animal on label & red flowers**."

With liquor and the pharmaceuticals dispersed, the people and furniture slid forward as the tilt increased. Then the room was ripped to pieces when the ship broke in two spilling everything out. Once we found where the Captain was we sought to determine if any of these details were verifiable. As mentioned in chapter one, we attempted to confirm McMoneagle's work by tracing White Star Lines pharmaceutical deliveries. The hope was to locate the supplier and get an old catalog that might show 1912 product pictures. Unfortunately, while every other ship store including the freight section had been scrutinized, we were blazing a new trail as no infirmary research existed. Again Harlan & Wolfe from Belfast:

Evidential Details

"I would suppose that White Star would have purchased their medical supplies from a pharmaceutical wholesaler in Southampton under a bulk purchase arrangement to cover all vessels."[xxvii]

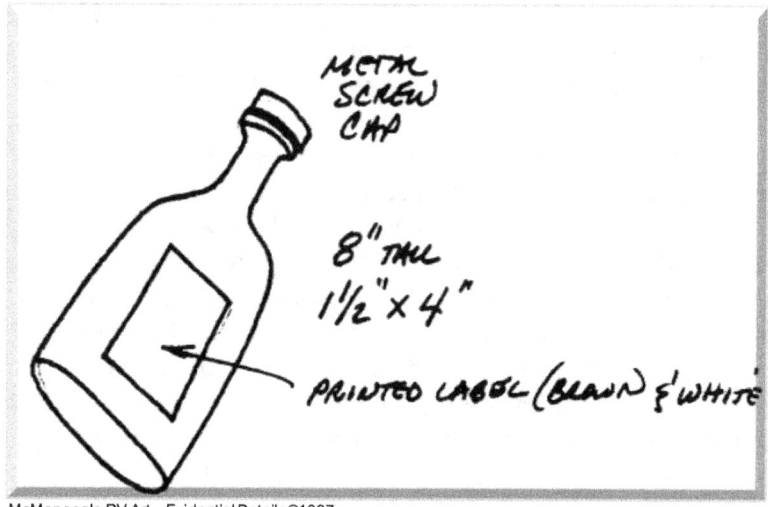

McMoneagle RV Art – Evidential Details©1997
The description reads: **Metal screw cap; 8" Tall; 1½" x 4"** (20.3 x 3.8 x 10.1cm); **Printed label (Brown & White)**

Salvage Discovery

Our being in receipt of pharmaceutical bottle drawings in January 1997, before these pieces were shown to the public would help authenticate – or dismiss – this material. So, we turned to salvage brought up by R.M.S. *Titanic*, Inc. Without comment, we submitted bottle drawings to the Curator of the *Titanic* Exhibition held in Memphis, Tennessee during August of that year. We asked if any of the drawings matched exhibit salvage realizing it would be better if a third party made the identification. In an informal telephone voice mail the Exposition's office acknowledged:

"We did have one of the bottles that looked similar. However, we don't have any other artifacts from the infirmary. And because of the way the artifacts spilled out, generally, we have found artifacts in groups. We have not found isolated artifacts - only one from each portion of the ship or anything like that. We have found for

Captain's Death

instance, hundreds of dishes and plates in one place. Considering we have not found any other medical equipment it is not likely that this one bottle that we have, that is similar to the one you had in the drawing, is indeed from the infirmary onboard the Titanic."

But in a follow-up phone call the curator told us the bottle was a match for one pictured in their *Titanic – The Exhibition* book. When we received a copy, the bottle was labeled as from the "dispensary".[xxviii] What seemed to be a declining statement fit perfectly. They thought infirmary equipment and medicinals should be found together just like the dish sets and the wine.

Due to their potency, infirmary medicines were locked away and should still be inside the ship's medicine cabinet below decks beyond the reach of salvagers. But bottles that were distributed to the passengers, emptied and then left in the First Class Smoking Lounge were by definition scattered. Their random bottle theory turned out to be entirely in keeping with the remote view! In fact, if the bottles were all found together – like the dishes - it would have been problematic. The stray empty pharmaceutical bottle is exactly what could be expected if the viewing was correct.

Just like the still corked wine bottles recovered, the pharmacy bottles were equally well capped in production and should still be sealed. Falling through water inside a medicine cabinet or a trunk would not open them. The circumstances of intact wine bottles and medicine bottles are the same. But salvage shows the medication bottles were opened, empty and dispersed.

If opened earlier, one would expect the proper disposal of these full strength narcotic containers. But scattered bottles indicates indifference to proper disposal. Given the drama of eminent death, it would have made no sense for the pharmaceuticals to stay in the medicine cabinet. That, **"numerous bottles and packages were hastily thrown into..."** the trunk also implies no previous preparation. Here we find group activity that emptied and scattered these bottles emerging as an evidential detail.

One skeptic alleged McMoneagle conducted turn of the century British pharmaceutical bottle shape research or that all his bottle drawings could have been pure luck because fewer bottle shapes existed at the time. Remembering that McMoneagle is only

Evidential Details

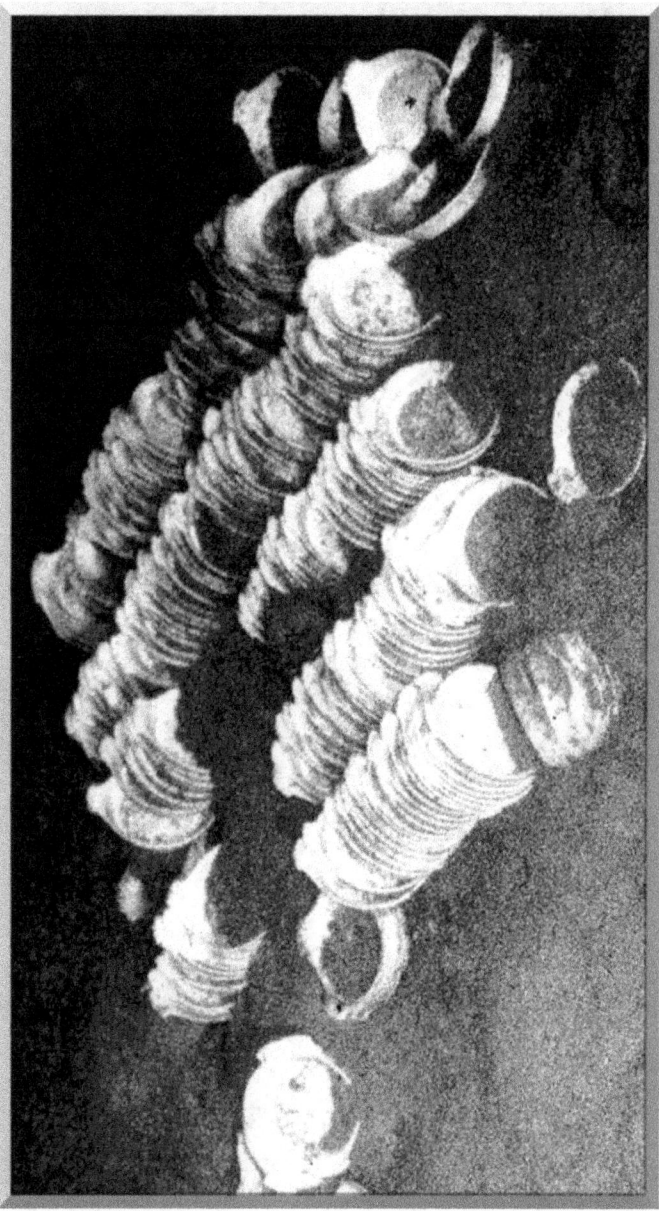

RMS *Titanic*, Inc.

"*Artifacts in groups*" Egg plates on the ocean floor provided an example of how *Titanic's* inventory came to rest. After a short voyage, the medicine bottles should still be full on the ocean floor or inside a locked F-deck medicine cabinet.

Captain's Death

Recovered Pharmacy Bottles

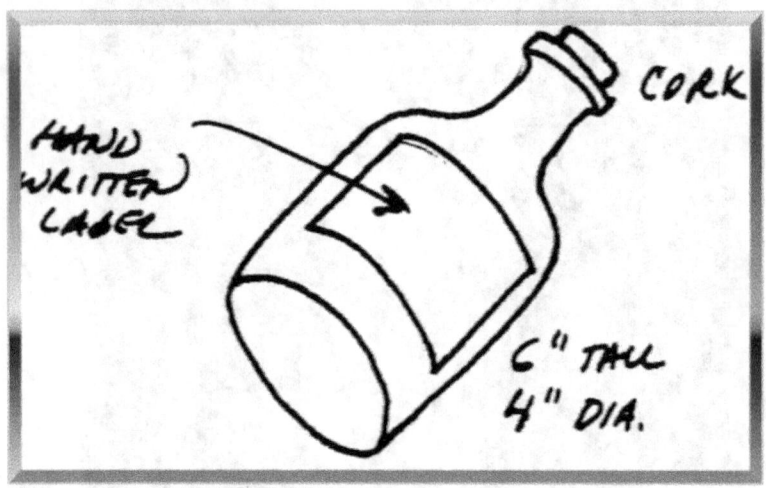

McMoneagle RV Art - Evidential Details ©1997

The bottle in question was drawn before the salvage bottles were first shown to the public.

RMS *Titanic*, Inc.

Such a bottle containing beige liquid did exist on the *Titanic* (middle) - salvaged post RV sessions. The tea bag bottle signifies first class British tidiness after pouring the drug. *Titanic's* drama asks the historian to contemplate the emotions of the wealthy, whose trembling lips last touched these bottle rims as the floor tore apart.

Evidential Details

looking at a double bind envelope, we went back and got this:

McMoneagle - ...there were a lot more bottle shapes back then than now, since most of the bottles were handmade.

It is now 1:50 am and the deck is listing to a severe 30 degrees. The forward (A) deck near the bow is nearly awash. There are small explosions occurring below decks, muffled by the water, which is now entering the large boiler sections in the forward steam rooms. I have a sense that the hot steam pipes are splitting when hit by the cold water flooding those areas. Much of the crew still below decks has been cut off from the upper deck areas.

The generator turbines probably operated throughout the sinking, which means every light on the ship was on - - even within the portions of the boat that were under water. It is now 2:00 am.

Not all the passengers are here. Some ...have chosen to return to their rooms where they locked themselves in. There are a few (perhaps a couple dozen) who have decided not to stay with the ship and are jumping from the side. Perhaps they have a fantasy that if they can swim to the lifeboats they could hold on until rescued, rather than go down with the ship. A useless thought, as none of them make it to any of the lifeboats. I sense some of the people in the lifeboats see them jumping and are turning away so as not to have to watch.

The Captain has tried to leave the passenger lounge to return to the upper deck, but he can no longer negotiate the passageways. So, he has elected to stay with the passengers who have remained in the lounge; fewer than half of the ones that originally gathered there. Most are now drinking heavily and contemplating their eventual deaths. The list is a full 40 degrees.

The Captain has elected to drink a full bottle of Laudanum which he consumes at approximately 2:10 am. I believe the Captain has opened a small flask, which he is now drinking heavily from. Normally he wouldn't be drinking hard liquor as he favors good wines and Port - - but he knows that

Captain's Death

his life will end swiftly in a few minutes. The ship is beginning to roll to one side now and many of the passengers are screaming and fighting to stay where they have previously... wedged their bodies.[11]

Harlan and Wolfe
With passengers toward the left, the tilt was actually toward the camera. Here the Smoking Lounge is shown from the other side, when the stern was in the air at 40°.

Some of the passengers are now dead having drunk a lethal mixture of alcohol and taken large doses of codeine or laudanum laced cough syrups or sleeping potions. Some of the passengers have injected full ampoules of Morphine but are still conscious.

The lights are beginning to fail throughout the boat. Power to the transmitters has just quit... A great deal of panic.

At approximately 2:18 am the ship begins to roll to the right while standing on its nose. Water is quickly flooding into the forward stations as water increases to spill into the rear

---

[11] Laudanum is not used in modern pain management. It is a tincture of opium in alcohol that was largely forgotten by the time of these sessions.

Evidential Details

holds. There are two large explosions below decks which are probably the main boilers (No's. 2 & 3) giving way. The Captain is no longer conscious. He and most of the other passengers are either dead or dying from the overdoses.

Once the ship began to roll it took less than three minutes for it to slide into the sea. I also have a sense there was a muffled explosion from somewhere below decks prior to the bow going completely under.

In the U.S. Hearings, Third Officer Pitman testified, "Then she turned right on end and went down perpendicularly." He said about the explosions, "They sounded like the reports of a big gun in the distance."

McMoneagle - There were a lot of interesting noises that accompanied the sinking. Probably from huge amounts of cargo that shifted forward, coal bunkers splitting, lots of breaking glass from inside the ship. My sense is that it was an awesome sight. The ship is shaken heavily by another muffled explosion, which can be heard by those in the lifeboats. This occurs after it has disappeared beneath the surface of the sea.

An eyewitness recalled, "It was like standing under a steel railway bridge while an express train passes overhead, mingled with the noise of a pressed-steel factory and wholesale breakage of china."[xxix] Such was the end of *Titanic*.

McMoneagle - The ship did sink bow first and this was observed by both Fleet and Lee. I see first one (Cunard Line *Carpathia*), **then a second large ship arriving on scene...** (White Star Lines *Olympic*). **Fleet was taken on board the first ship... My sense is that both vessels were bound for England.**[12]

After the disaster was reported, the cable laying ship *Mackay Bennett* was dispatched to gather bodies. The undertaker of Snow & Company brought 100 coffins and all the embalming fluid in Halifax, Nova Scotia. Three hundred and six corpses would be retrieved of which 116 were buried at sea. From the ship's railing seamen recalled that the floating bodies:

---

[12] The *Carpathia* was originally sailing to Gibraltar. It was sunk by a German U-boat on July 17, 1918, just 17 weeks before the end of World War One.

Captain's Death

"...seemed like a great flock of gulls on the water, bobbing gently in the swell. They were all floating in an upright position as if treading water, most of them in a greater cluster in amongst and surrounded by small debris, many faces distorted by terror, so reports went, clutching clothes or objects which they had grasped at in their agony - others with their legs or bodies mangled as if by an explosion."xxx There had been blood in the water.

Photographer Unknown
With the suspected iceberg in the background, here the historian can get an idea of the pitch black ice water over 1500 passengers went into along with Titanic's debris.

Other ships picked-up macabrously configured corpses. One man was floating dead on a door. A woman was found in her nightgown which had billowed out on to the water's surface. Some were found sitting in floating wooden chairs. There was a young mother with a tormented infant frozen into her arms. The total number of survivors and recovered bodies totaled approximately 1,043, which accounted for less than half of the people on board.

Evidential Details

In the end, *Titanic's* new life jackets created the most misery. Consider that the average passenger had gone from sleeping in a warm bed to alarmed confusion, to dread, to the terror of plunging into pitch black ice water. Then the second calamity of encountering a cruelly tranquil sea that prevented drowning thus prolonging the death struggle. Somewhat the reverse of being burned alive, subfreezing salt water immersion is the suspended animation of brutally invasive body agony.

As the ship's aft section slid into the water beautifully starlit heavens beheld a frigid flailing. Trapped innocents were eventually pressed from shock to lunatic delirium as they bumped along in the maniacal screaming chaos of the heavily debrided pitch black. In this excruciating full body agony, anyone would wish to die sooner than later. But most, unable to inhale salt brine, became the countdown beholders of the final seconds their energy was frozen right out of their body. Moment by moment each tender rumination went mote and was forever lost into the hew.

In a letter from the *New York World*, correspondent H.C. Wolfe told the Disaster Hearings a steamer called the *Minia* arrived in Halifax, Nova Scotia on May 6 with fifteen of the seventeen bodies they recovered. Two had been buried at sea. A lung exam of all seventeen revealed only one had drown.

* * *

White Star Lines Managing Director Joseph Bruce Ismay (1862-1936) will be forever reviled for having survived the disaster. He had seen the 1:42 p.m. ice warning from the *S.S. Baltic* and still, once he had engineering approval, authorized two more boilers to be brought on while influencing the Captain to increase speed as they headed toward the ice field.

No other Corporate Director has ever been reduced from the luxury of a $50,000 (US$ 1997) First Class suite to bobbing at sea in a crowded lifeboat in just over two hours. And even though three lifeboats had, "very dim, small lamps"[xxxi] few people today have a chance to experience the type of total darkness the fearfully sullen Ismay found himself.

As the ship foundered the yelling, screaming and crying

Captain's Death

out of hundreds of men, women and children haunted him. The resonance would have been one of hearing hundreds, of all ages and genders, being simultaneously stabbed with a small penknife for 5 to 15 minutes until dead. He knew he had played a role and did not look back. With some hard tack biscuits, little fresh water, and no toilet privacy in a crowd of twenty-eight women and ten third class men, Ismay's reality was transformed like no other Managing Director in history. As the senior survivor, he had time to think as he rolled and drifted in the twinkling blackness uncertain how long he would be at sea in his slippers and pajamas under his suit. In the end, 705 passengers were saved. But with a life boat capacity of 1178, they were less than 60% utilized.

Once onboard the *Carpathia* Ismay retired to the physician's cabin. He told the Committee:

Ismay - "I think the Captain of the *Carpathia* is here, and he will probably tell you that I was never out of my room from the time I got on board the *Carpathia* until the ship docked here last night. I never moved out of the room."[xxxii] With good reason.

After a visit John Thayer recalled, "I have never seen a man so completely wrecked. Nothing I could say or do brought any response."[xxxiii] Ismay may have been given opium to easy him psychologically. But there was more than the sinking to be concerned with. He focused on liability.

J. Bruce Ismay was to sustain an incredible amount of public scorn that turn of the century British upper class had no experience coping with. Panicked personality aside in a needed historical reinterpretation, Ismay can almost be seen as a hapless character forced into a lifelong protector for what he considered undeserving bunglers. After a grueling examination by the Americans, he was released to return to England on Tuesday, April 30.

Once in England Ismay needed to be solicitous of sailors protected by an immensely powerful union. For corporate liability purposes, he could not allow these men to turn on him as it was management (2nd Officer Lightoller) who had given the men permission to leave the crow's nest. And it was management (First Officer Murdoch) that had taken no action on ice warnings.

Ismay is said to have delivered payoffs to be certain of tes-

Evidential Details

Illustrated London News

Quiet, White Star Lines Managing Director J. Bruce Ismay (hand to mouth) pondered what to say in New York's Waldorf Astoria East Room. Worried about the whole scenario being unmasked, he considered every word for what would be referenced in the British Hearings. Unknown before this book is that he went on to orchestrate the greatest maritime disaster cover-up in world history.

Captain's Death

timonial consistency between the two hearings. Then he had to live out his life protecting those lies. And, in spite of his success, once the loose ends were attended to, Harold Sanderson replaced him fourteen months after the British Hearings ended.

With time J. Bruce Ismay realized he would be written into history as the villain of the whole *Titanic* affair. It was however critical the lookouts be represented as blameless. They had the ability to turn on ship's officers for granting permission to leave the crow's nest against regulations while running full speed in an ice field.

Then there was the awareness Quartermaster Hitchens had to reverse direction. It must have been a severe daily frustration for Ismay to realize he had to coach a cover-up that made him the fall guy. But Ismay was in a delicate situation facing possible imprisonment and corporate ruin.

His response was one of private ire to his new life whose circumstances had been transformed overnight. He banned all reference to the *Titanic* in his presence. Just like Frederick Fleet's 1964 slip, Ismay could have inferred something casting doubt on his earlier statements. In the end, he would be forced into the pathetic role of preservationist of an odious case against himself for all time which was his punishment in lieu of imprisonment. Good in sports, an avid fisherman and a thoroughly competitive businessman, one can only stop to reflect that except for remote viewing, the truth would never have been uncovered.

Curiously, when we contacted the Ismay family with news that a reinterpretation of their great grandfather was in order, they were hushed. Remote viewing was not mentioned, but some of our conclusions were. With all the abuse heaped upon their ancestor one would think that any reinterpretation would want to be reviewed. Why remain silent when this new data was offered freely?

If the Ismay family knows more about these private circumstances it would seem that a century is enough time to permit a release of information, for we know now there was no way for the truth to come out. While no self-serving critic has ever said they would be willing to trade places with Ismay eyeing the last life boat, the irony is that by not accepting a horribly slow death, J. Bruce Ismay became the spider that ate the poison fly of life.

Evidential Details

* * *

Owing to financial losses during the Great Depression the British government offered White Star and Cunard Lines the amount of £ 9.5 million if they would merge. The merger took place in 1934 with Cunard gaining a 62% share of the corporate stock.

During the feedback session in which the target was revealed to McMoneagle, a question arose about the *Titanic's* records. Not surprisingly, "According to the National Maritime Museum at Greenwich, even the White Star's company records have vanished." And,"...since no *Titanic* provisioning list survives...""[xxxiv] we asked about it.

McMoneagle - As regards the records of the *Titanic*, specifically the provisioning records... I have a sense the originals were maintained by the White Star Headquarters. These records were stored formally in the Headquarters offices for many years. I have a sense they were kept in boxes that were relegated to the basement of the building. These records were destroyed when the original Headquarters was bought and changed hands...

In 1947, Cunard bought White Star out and merged or liquidated most of its holdings. This is probably the year the original office records were destroyed. If not, then certainly when White Star Line was liquidated at midnight December 31, 1949. But:

McMoneagle - There were copies of these records which were kept on file by the accounting firm hired by the White Star Line to manage their financial records. I believe some of these copies still exist (1997). **You need to identify the accounting firm, who it** (they) **were sold to, and what it is known as today. I don't believe they know they have these records, as they are a part of the historical files they have stored in a warehouse separate from their current operations.**

Titanic crashed into the ocean floor on the Newfoundland Ridge just south of the ocean floor's Grand Bank drop east of the Laurentian Cone at 41°43'57" N - 49°56'49" W. The stern and the bow sections lie approximately 1970 feet (600m) apart. It is estimated it took five minutes for the bow to angle down into the ocean floor where it dug in some 18 feet deep. The ship's bow lies in

Captain's Death

12,434 feet (3,789.8m) of water, and the stern at 12,451 feet (3,795m). Two other hull sections have also been found.

Now, through remote viewing, historians can observe the true chain of events. A resigning Captain was pushed to go near full speed into a known ice field by a non-maritime corporate executive who had full confidence in the captain's abilities. The ocean was strangely calm and the air was at near record low temperature. A sympathetic Second Officer overrode regulations and allowed the crow's nest to be temporarily half staffed. After warning the bridge three times, the ice side lookout acted on the work rule exception precisely as the berg approached. The First Officer inexplicably ignored the ice warnings and then gave the helmsman countermanding steering orders insuring a lengthened impact tear. The directly accountable ship's management all died. The hands-on union men all lived.

As regards the court records of the British and American investigations the renowned *Titanic* author Walter Lord, from whose book the 1958 movie was made, pointed out: "There are 181 witness and 2,111 pages of testimony. Some of it ambiguous, inconsistent, and even contradictory. These gleanings may prove useful, if only because they show it is hard to corner that elusive quarry, the truth."[xxxv]

The White Star Line five point star on the trunk drawn by McMoneagle (p. 122).

Note: Some entries below are abbreviated references from the first chapter.

[i] Testimony - Managing Director J. Bruce Ismay; Friday, April 19, 1912 in the Waldorf Astoria East Room, New York, New York.
[ii] Marcus, Geoffrey; *The Maiden Voyage*; The Viking Press 1969 p 39; *Gardner;*

Evidential Details

[ii] p.48; Wade; p.48
[iii] Lord, Walter; *The Night Lives On*; William Morrow and Co.; 1986; p.38,
[iv] *Gardner*; p. 49
[v] Tresh, Peter; *Titanic - The Truth Behind the Disaster*; Crescent Books; 1992; p. 28,
[vi] Marcus; p. 40
[vi] Stenson, Patrick; p. 144
[vii] The *Titanic Disaster Hearings before a Subcommittee on Commerce - United States Senate*; Sixty-Second Congress, Second Edition pursuant to Senate resolution 283; Directing the Committee on Commerce to Investigate the Causes Leading to the Wreck of the White Star Liner *"Titanic"*. Washington Government Printing Office 1912; Testimony of Frederick D. Ray; First Class Dining Room Steward; hereafter referred to as SH.
[ix] Affidavit submitted to the Senate Disaster Subcommittee by Eleanor Widener; Sworn to on the 29th day of May, 1912.
[x] Stenson; p. 167
[xi] Marcus; p. 209
[xi] Testimony - rescue ship *Carpathia* wireless operator Harold Thomas Cottam; Friday, April 19, 1912; Waldorf Astoria East Room, New York, New York
[xii] SH; Testimony of Guglielmo Marconi; Thursday, April 25, 1912
[xiv] SH; Testimony of Frederick M. Sammis, General Manager, Marconi Wireless Telegraph Company of America; Monday, April 29, 1912
[xv] The *New York Times*, Friday April 19, 1912 entitled, *Thrilling Story by Titanic's Surviving Wireless Man*.
[xvi] OT; p. 77
[xvi] Senate Commerce Committee's Disaster subcommittee regarding the final report on the *Titanic* dated May 28, 1912 entitled, "Investigation into the Loss of S.S. *Titanic*."; Report pursuant to Senate resolution 283.
[xvii] SH; Testimony - Harold Bride, Saturday, April 20, 1912; Waldorf Astoria East Room, New York, New York
[xix] www.encyclopedia-*Titanic*a.org;
[xx] SH; Testimony - Henry Samuel Etches, Bedroom Steward; Saturday April 27, 1912
[xxi] Quinn, Paul J.; *Titanic at Two A.M.*; Fantail Publishing; 1997; p. 84.
[xxi] Marcus; p. 40
[xxii] Pellegrino, Charles; *Her Name Titanic*; McGraw-Hill Publishing, 1988; pp. 111 – 113
[xxiv] Tresh; p. 60
[xxv] Quinn; p. 66-67
[xxvi] *Wade;* p.208
[xxvii] E-mail correspondence with hrtech.serv, dated March 7, 1997
[xxviii] *Titanic – The Exhibition*; Wonders, The Memphis International Cultural Series, A Division of the City of Memphis, Tennessee in association with RMS *Titanic*, Inc. 1997; p. 89
[xxix] Wade; 209
[xxx] Padfield; p.181
[xxxi] SH; Testimony - Fourth Officer Joseph Groves Boxhall
[xxxi] Testimony, Managing Director J. Bruce Ismay Friday, April 19, 1912 Waldorf Astoria East Room, New York, New York
[xxxiii] Davie; p 122
[xxxiv] Gardner; p. 43 quoting a Robin Gardener letter - March 18, 1944 p. 63
[xxxv] Lord; last two quotations p. 241

Evidential Details

BIBLIOGRAPHY

- Davie, Michael, *Titanic - The Death and Life of a Legend*; Alfred A. Knopf, Inc.; 1986;
- Freud, Sigmund, *The Complete Introductory Lectures on Psychoanalysis*; translated and edited by James Strachey; W.W. Norton & Company, Inc. 1966;
- Gardner, Robin and Dan Van der Vat, *The Titanic Conspiracy*; Carol Publishing Group; 1995;
- Harlan & Wolff's Offices; e-mail correspondence with hrtech.serv, May, 1997;
- Her Majesties Coroner David C. Horsley's Office, Portsmouth & South East Hampshire
- Lord, Walter; *The Night Lives On*; William Morrow and Co.; 1986;
- Marcus, Geoffrey; *The Maiden Voyage*; The Viking Press 1969;
- Office of the Highland Road Cemetery;
- Padfield, Peter, *The Titanic and the Californian*; John Day Company; 1965;
- Pellegrino, Charles; *Her Name Titanic*; McGraw-Hill Publishing, 1988;
- Quinn, Paul J.; *Titanic at Two A.M.*; Fantail Publishing; 1997;
- Reade, Leslie, *The Ship That Stood Still*; W. W. Norton & Company, Inc.; 1993;
- Senate Commerce Committee's Disaster subcommittee regarding the final report on the *Titanic* dated May 28, 1912 entitled, "Investigation into the Loss of S.S. *Titanic*."; Report pursuant to Senate resolution 283.
- Stenson, Patrick, *The Odyssey of C.H. Lightoller*, W.W. Norton & Company; 1984;
- The *Titanic Disaster Hearings before a Subcommittee on Commerce - United States Senate*; Sixty-Second Congress, Second Edition pursuant to Senate resolution 283; Directing the Committee on Commerce to Investigate the Causes Leading to the Wreck of the White Star Liner "*Titanic*". Washington Government Printing Office 1912;
- *Titanic – The Exhibition*; Wonders, The Memphis International Cultural Series, A Division of the City of Memphis, Tennessee in association with RMS *Titanic*, Inc. 1997;
- Tresh, Peter; *Titanic - The Truth Behind the Disaster*; Crescent Books; 1992;
- Wade, Wyn Craig, *The Titanic - End of a Dream*; Rawson, Wade Publishers, Inc. 1979;

NEWSPAPERS – WEB SITES

- The *New York Times*, Friday April 19, 1912, *Thrilling Story by Titanic's Surviving Wireless Man*.
- The *New York Times*, Sunday, April 23, 1912

- www.*Titanic*inquiry.org; © 1999-2007 *Titanic* Inquiry Project
- www.encyclopedia-*Titanica*.org;
- www.friendsofhighlandroadcemetery.org.uk Copyright © 2011 CIS/FOHRC

Evidential Details

Part III

...as a result of my own previous exposure to this (remote viewing) *community I became persuaded that war can almost always be traced to a failure in intelligence, and that therefore the strongest weapon for peace is good intelligence.*

~ H. E. Puthoff, PhD. ~

Founder and First Director (1972 - 1985)
The U.S. Military Intelligence program
known as Operation Star Gate

Evidential Details

Credentials

JOSEPH W. MCMONEAGLE, CW2, US Army, Ret., KCStS
Owner/Executive Director of
Intuitive Intelligence Applications, Inc.

Mr. McMoneagle has over 45 years of professional expertise in research and development, in numerous multi-level technical systems, the paranormal, and the social sciences. Experience includes: experimental protocol design, collection and evaluation of statistical information, prototype design and testing, Automatic Data Processing equipment and technology interface, management, and data systems analysis for mainframe, mini-mainframe, and desktop computer systems supporting information collection and analysis for intelligence purposes.

He is currently owner and Executive Director of Intuitive Intelligence Applications, Inc., which has provided support to multiple research facilities and corporations with a full range of collection applications using Anomalous Cognition (AC) in the production of original and cutting edge information. He is a full time Research Associate with The Laboratories for Fundamental Research, Cognitive Sciences Laboratory, Palo Alto, California, where he has provided consulting support to research and development in remote viewing for 16+ years. As a consultant to SRI-International and Science Applications International Corporation, Inc. from 1984 through 1995, he participated in protocol design, statistical information collection, R&D evaluations, as well as thousands of remote viewing trials in support of both experimental research and active intelligence operations for what is now known as Project STARGATE. He is well versed with developmental theory, methods of application, and current training technologies for remote viewing, as currently applied under strict laboratory controls and oversight.

During his career, Mr. McMoneagle has provided professional intelligence and creative/innovative informational support to the Central Intelligence Agency, Defense Intelligence

Credentials

Agency, National Security Agency, Drug Enforcement Agency, Secret Service, Federal Bureau of Investigation, United States Customs, the National Security Council, most major commands within the Department of Defense, and hundreds of other individuals, companies, and corporations. He is the only one who has successfully demonstrated his ability more than two dozen times, by doing a live remote viewing, double-blind and under controls while on-camera for national networks/labs in four countries.

Mr. McMoneagle has also been responsible for his Military Occupational Specialty at Army Headquarters level, to include control and management of both manned and unmanned sites within the Continental United States, and overseas. He was responsible for all tactical and strategic equipment tasking, including aircraft and vehicles, development of new and current technology, planning, support and maintenance, funding, training, and personnel. He has performed responsibly in international and intra-service negotiations and agreements in support of six national level intelligence agencies, and has acted as a direct consultant to the Commanding General, United States Army Intelligence and Security Command (INSCOM), Washington D.C., as well as the Army Chief of Staff for Intelligence (ACSI), Pentagon.

"For the intelligence world, mental access of target people has great value. Profilers and psychological analysts who specialize in this craft are highly prized within the intelligence community. They are employed in that part of the intelligence community which is called HUMINT, which is short for "Human Intelligence," or "intelligence derived from human sources."

Lyn Buchanan – *The Seventh Sense*

Evidential Details

Human Use

Sometimes Remote Viewing research requires input from different sources as in this example about the Army's Human Use policies.

"In February 1979, the General Counsel, the Army's top lawyer, declared [RV Code Name] Grill Flame activities constitute Human Use." The Unit, "... was in the middle of the [authorization] process in March 1979 when the Human Use determination was reversed by the Army Surgeon General's Human Use Subjects Research Review Board. Their decision...trumped the Army General Counsel's ruling..." "On November 20, the Surgeon General's board changed its mind and decided that Grill Flame did indeed involve Human Use. It took until February 1, 1982 to get final approval from the Secretary of the Army to continue operations." [1]

Candidates were then given a warning by a Major General before being accepted into the super secret 902nd Intelligence Unit.

"Among other things, they noted that if he joined the project, he would be exposed to psychic phenomena at a level and with a frequency that most people had never experienced before. As a result, he might change in certain ways. Ultimately, no harm should come to him, but he might have a new perspective on himself, his marriage, the universe. In a sense, he might become a new man, and a new husband."

The candidate and his wife were advised to talk, "...this over before they made the final commitment to go to Fort Meade." [2]

---

[1] Smith, Paul H., *Reading the Enemy's Mind – Inside Star Gate, America's Psychic Espionage Program*; Tor Non-fiction, 2005; p. 118

[2] Schnabel, Jim, *Remote Viewers: The Secret History of America's Psychic Spies*; Dell Non-Fiction, 1997, p. 270

Evidential Details

A CHINESE ENCOUNTER

The United States is not the only nation to study and use Remote Viewing. Below is a story allowing enthusiasts and skeptics alike a rare look at life inside the Unit during the middle 1980's.

The first time it happened was right after [Major] General Stubblebine had briefed me on the project and said that I would be contacted. The next week I was working mid shift, and one of the afternoons, I lay down for a nap. In that nap, I had a really shallow and lame dream about something I can't remember now. But at one point, right over the top of that dream there was what appeared to be a semi-translucent visual of three people. One was a very respectable, businesslike slender man in a suit. A second was a very burly, stocky man, also in a suit, and with a very "Texas farmer" face. The third was an...oriental girl... (I find it impossible to tell the age of oriental women). She was following along behind the two men and watching. The men came up to me and talked about something, but I couldn't hear them. The girl was standing behind the two men, listening. The faces were very clear. Clear enough that when the two men actually came to [the INSCOM[1] Base in] Augsburg [Germany] to interview me, I recognized them immediately. I could have picked them out of a crowd on the sidewalk. I didn't think anything of the fact that the girl wasn't with them. It would have been odd to have her on a military trip overseas. I thought she was probably someone in the unit. Months later, when I got to the unit, she wasn't there. I asked about her and neither the director nor Joe [McMoneagle] (the two men who came to interview me) knew who I was talking about. I figured that it was just an AOL (STRAY CAT),[2] and blew it off.

About a year later, I was doing a practice target. The target was a museum at Arizona State University (I didn't know that - I only had

---

[1] INSCOM is the abbreviation for the Army's Intelligence and Security Command.
[2] Stray Cat is a viewer acronym describing the Subconscious Transfer of Recollections, Anxieties, and Yearnings to Consciously Accessible Thought.

Chinese Encounter

numbers). I was describing things lying in glass-topped cases, with the cases up on legs and stands, all arranged around the room for easy access, when I noticed that someone at the target site was looking straight at me, as though she could see me. It startled me, and for probably the only time ever, I wasn't startled OUT of the session, but deeper into it. I looked back at her, and realized that it was the same girl who had been following the director and Joe in my earlier "dream", back in Augsburg. I looked directly at her, and started to say hello, but then she realized that I could see her, too, and she half turned, and disappeared. That threw me out of the session. Fortunately, [Captain] Paul Smith was my monitor, and ever the curious one, when I told him what had happened, he said, "Let's follow her and see where she went." Through a series of very impromptu movement commands, we finally located her back at the place where she worked ... the Chinese psychic intelligence effort.

She appeared in some of my sessions after that, but rarely. I tried to find her several times, and a few of them succeeded. Apparently, what they defined as "session" and what we defined as "session" weren't the same. Anyway, over time, we struck up somewhat of a stand-offish acquaintance. About a year after that, I hadn't bumped into her again, so I did a session specifically to find her. She was then in college in a very large city, and evidently out of the government's project altogether. When I found her, she acknowledged my presence, and very strongly desired that we not have further contact. I backed out of the session, and haven't tried again, since. Don't cha love war stories?" [3]

> Oct. 1, 1998 e-mail from Leonard Buchanan – Former Operational Database Manager 902nd Military Intelligence Unit - Fort Meade, Maryland and Owner of Problems>Solutions>Innovations, Inc.

---

[3] For more information, see, *China's Super Psychics* by Paul Dong and Thomas Raffill; Marlowe & Co. New York, 1997

Evidential Details

Remote Viewing Protocols

Surrounding the military's RV session protocols are the Operational Flow Protocols. The tasking agency was the "Customer" whose identity was strictly withheld to avoid inferences leading to Analytic Overlay. First published here, this process was highly classified for over two decades.

* * *

"In actual fact, there was pretty much a different work set-up every time we changed directors in the military unit which was pretty often as projects go. As a result, the "ideal plan" was never adhered to. Many times, we had to sort of switch horse in mid-stream. Anyway, here is the "ideal" workflow:

The **CUSTOMER** (Governmental Agency) comes to the unit director with a tasking.
The **UNIT DIRECTOR** meets with the customer and:
1) makes absolutely certain that the customer knows what CRV is and isn't – what it will and won't do.
2) looks the customer's problem over to see that it is the type of work we are best suited for. If not, he suggests a different solution for them.
If so, he then:
3) gets rid of the customer's "test" questions which only take up time and effort and accomplish nothing.
4) gets rid of the unnecessary questions – just fluff questions which the customer would like to have answered.
5) makes certain the questions asked are questions the customer really wants the answers to. There are LOTS of times when the customer will ask, "Who killed the victim", when the information he really wants is, "Where can we find the evidence that will show who killed the victim?"
6) agrees in writing on a set of basic questions which will be answered, once all the fluff and confusion is gotten out of the way.
7) makes certain that the Customer knows that these questions will

Protocols

be answered, and that other information will be provided, if it is found. However, if it isn't found, then the viewers are only responsible for what is being tasked. Follow-on questions will have to be asked later.

8) explains to the Customer the need for accurate feedback.

9) gets a definite commitment from the Customer that such feedback will be given, on each and every viewer's answer(s) to each and every question.

10) sets a commitment date for providing the answers. This must be a realistic date. Every Customer wants answers right now or yesterday, but the unit director needs to impress on the Customer that there are other customers who also have time limits of now or yesterday, and that reality must figure into the planning, like it or not.

11) provides the final list of questions to the Project Officer, along with any background information about the case gained from the customer.

The **PROJECT OFFICER** studies the background information and tasked questions and:

1) determines the main subject matter for each question.

2) decides the project number and fills out all the preliminary paperwork required for starting a new project.

3) provides the list of subjects to the Data Base Manager. The Data Base Manager looks up each information category in the data base and provides the Project Manager with a separate list of Viewers' names as suggested Viewers for each question.

4) determines which Viewers and Monitors should work on each question.

5) looks at the Viewers' and Monitors' existing schedules and determines the project's time line. He may even do a Pert chart to make scheduling easier.

6) "translates" each question into neutral wording.

7) notifies each Monitor and Viewer of the work schedule change.

8) generates an official tasking sheet to hand to each Monitor.

Evidential Details

The **MONITOR** receives the tasking and coordinates from the Project Officer, along with any background information the Project Officer thinks the Monitor should know to help the Viewer better perform a productive session. The Monitor then:
1) makes certain he knows the Viewer's likes and dislikes, quirks, micro-movements, etc. If not, these are either looked up or found out from another Monitor who is more familiar with the Viewer.
2) gets information from the Database Manager about the Viewer's strengths and weaknesses. While this carries the danger of a "self-fulfilling prophecy", the Monitor is hopefully trained enough to use the information for formatting the session, rather than for guiding and leading the Viewer. If the Monitor is not this well trained, this step is passed up.
3) prepares the session workplace.
4) goes through the session with the Viewer.
5) helps the Viewer write the summary, if necessary.
6) after the paperwork is all done, provides both the Viewer's transcript and his (the Monitor's) session notes to the Analyst.

The **ANALYST** receives the paperwork and:
1) familiarizes himself with all the background knowledge.
2) collects the papers from all Viewer/Monitor pairs.
3) looks into his own notes on each and every Viewer to see work profiles (prone to using imagery, prone to using allegories, etc.). The Database Manager can be of help in this step.
4) performs analysis on the session (see the Analyst's Manual).
5) writes up his reports, critiques, summaries, etc. and provides it to the Report Writer.

The **REPORT WRITER** receives all the information from the Analyst and:
1) familiarizes himself with all the available background information.
2) familiarizes himself with all the Analyst's finding, interpretations and comments.
3) writes the final report (see the Report Writer's Manual)

Protocols

NOTE!!! This includes taking the finalized answer to each Viewer to make certain that what is being reported is what the Viewer actually meant to say.
4) provides the final report to the Project Officer.

The **PROJECT OFFICER** then:
1) receives the finalized answers to each question after the session has been performed, analyzed and prepared for reporting.
2) gives final approval on the final report.
3) passes the final report to the Unit Director for delivery to the Customer.

The **UNIT DIRECTOR** then:
1) contacts the Customer and sets a date and time to go over the report. Information is not given ad hoc over the phone, nor is an "executive summary" provided.
2) meets with the Customer to provide the report.
3) once again makes certain that the Customer understands the CRV process, strengths and limitations.
4) explains what happened, and how each answer was obtained.
5) points out to the Customer that each question has a "dependability rating" beside it which will tell the Customer what each Viewer's track record is on each specific answer to each type of question. He explains how this "dependability rating" can be used by the Customer as an aid to making decisions from the information provided.
6) sets – in writing – a hard and definite "drop dead" date for feedback.
7) if/when feedback comes in, provides it to the Project Officer who handled the case.
8) if feedback doesn't come in, or is received incorrectly, it is returned to the Customer to either, "dun him" for feedback, or to re-explain how feed-back needs to be provided, formatted, etc.

The **PROJECT OFFICER** then:
1) evaluates each Viewer's response to each question against the feedback.

Evidential Details

2) provides an evaluation to each Viewer.
3) provides accurate data to the Database Manager for input into the database.
4) completes all summary paperwork for the project.
5) organizes all related paperwork, checks it for completeness, and prepares it for final storage and filing.

The **DATABASE MANAGER**:
1) inputs all received information into the database.
2) "massages" the database to provide information to those who need it. This includes the Training Officer and all Trainers.
3) maintains quality control on the data going in. "Garbage in – garbage out".

The **TRAINING OFFICER**:
1) schedules training times and facilities.
2) keeps evaluation reports on the Trainers.

The **TRAINER**:
1) accompanies new Viewers through the training process, analyzing their needs and progress every step of the way (see Trainers Manual).
2) makes and keeps records of the Viewer Student's "natural micro-movements". These will be provided to the Monitors along with a Viewer Student's profile of strengths and weakness.
3) advises management of the Viewer Student's progress and advises as to the student's best possible "training track" for providing the most useful and productive Viewer possible.

Needless to say, this is an overview, and not a complete list of responsibilities and obligations. For example, it doesn't cover what goes on in follow-on tasking, etc.

July 23, 1998 e-mail from: Leonard Buchanan– Former Operational Database Manager at the 902nd Military Intelligence Unit - Fort Meade, Maryland and Owner of Problems> Solutions>Innovations, Inc.

"The 'giggle factor' associated with remote viewing or psychic functioning continues to block earnest attempts at using these functions for humankind's benefit." - Joseph McMoneagle

Evidential Details

Beginnings

This details the basis for the original black ops program funding. For readers interested in the data that justified more Congressional spending, this secretive overview of U.S. Military History is recommended.

CIA-Initiated Remote Viewing At Stanford Research Institute

by H. E. Puthoff, Ph.D.[1]
Institute for Advanced Studies at Austin
4030 Braker Lane W., #300
Austin, Texas 78759-5329

Abstract - In July 1995 the CIA declassified, and approved for release, documents revealing its sponsorship in the 1970s of a program at Stanford Research Institute in Menlo Park, CA, to determine whether such phenomena as remote viewing "might have any utility for intelligence collection" [1]. Thus began disclosure to the public of a two-decade-plus involvement of the intelligence community in the investigation of so-called para-psychological or psi phenomena. Presented here by the program's Founder and first Director (1972 - 1985) is the early history of the program, including discussion of some of the first, now declassified, results that drove early interest.

---

[1]Harold Puthoff received his BS and MS Degrees in Electrical Engineering at the University of Florida and a PhD from Stanford University in 1967. He went on to work at the National Security Agency at Fort Meade, Maryland as an Army engineer studying, lasers, high-speed computers, and fiber optics. He is the inventor of the tunable infra-red laser. He spent three years as a naval officer and worked eight years in the Microwave Laboratory at Stanford. Puthoff has over 31 technical papers published on such topics as electron-beam devices, lasers and quantum zero-point-energy effects. He reportedly has patents issued in the areas of energy fields, laser, and communications. [author]

Beginnings

Introduction

On April 17, 1995, President Clinton issued Executive Order Nr. 1995-4-17, entitled Classified National Security Information. Although in one sense the order simply reaffirmed much of what has been long-standing policy, in another sense there was a clear shift toward more openness. In the opening paragraph, for example, we read: "In recent years, however, dramatic changes have altered, although not eliminated, the national security threats that we confront. These changes provide a greater opportunity to emphasize our commitment to open Government." In the Classification Standards section of the Order this commitment is operationalized by phrases such as "If there is significant doubt about the need to classify information, it shall not be classified." Later in the document, in reference to information that requires continued protection, there even appears the remarkable phrase "In some exceptional cases, however, the need to protect such information may be outweighed by the public interest in disclosure of the information, and in these cases the information should be declassified."

A major fallout of this reframing of attitude toward classification is that there is enormous pressure on those charged with maintaining security to work hard at being responsive to reasonable requests for disclosure. One of the results is that FOIA (Freedom of Information Act) requests that have languished for months to years are suddenly being acted upon.[1]

One outcome of this change in policy is the government's recent admission of its two-decade-plus involvement in funding highly-classified, special access programs in remote viewing (RV) and related psi phenomena, first at Stanford Research Institute (SRI) and then at Science Applications International Corporation (SAIC), both in Menlo Park, CA, supplemented by various in-house government programs. Although almost all of the documentation remains yet classified, in July 1995 270 pages of SRI reports were declassified and released by the CIA, the program's first sponsor [2]. Thus, although through the years columns by Jack Anderson and others had claimed leaks of "psychic spy" programs with such exotic names as Grill Flame, Center Lane, Sunstreak and Star Gate, CIA's release of the SRI reports constitutes the first documented public admission of significant intelligence community involvement in the psi area.

As a consequence of the above, although I had founded the program in early 1972, and had acted as its Director until I left in 1985 to head up the Institute for Advanced Studies at Austin (at which point my colleague Ed May assumed responsibility as Director), it was not until 1995 that I found myself for the first time able to utter in a single sentence the connected acronyms CIA/SRI/RV. In this report I discuss the genesis of the program, report on some of the early, now declassified, results that drove early interest, and outline the general direction the program took as it expanded into a multi-year, multi-site, multi-million-dollar effort to determine whether such phenomena as remote viewing "might have any utility for intelligence collection" [1].

Beginnings

In early 1972, I was involved in laser research at Stanford Research Institute (now called SRI International) in Menlo Park, CA. At that time I was also circulating a proposal to obtain a small grant for some research in quantum biology. In that proposal I had raised the issue whether physical theory as we knew it was capable of describing life processes, and had suggested some measurements involving plants and lower organisms [3]. This proposal was widely circulated, and a copy was sent to Cleve Backster in New York City who was involved in measuring the electrical activity of plants with standard polygraph equipment. New York artist Ingo Swann chanced to see my proposal during a visit to Backster's lab, and wrote me suggesting that if I were interested in investigating the boundary between the physics of the

Beginnings

animate and inanimate, I should consider experiments of the parapsychological type. Swann then went on to describe some apparently successful experiments in psychokinesis in which he had participated at Prof. Gertrude Schmeidler's laboratory at the City College of New York. As a result of this correspondence I invited him to visit SRI for a week in June 1972 to demonstrate such effects, frankly, as much out of personal scientific curiosity as anything else.

Prior to Swann's visit I arranged for access to a well-shielded magneto-meter used in a quark-detection experiment in the Physics Department at Stanford University. During our visit to this laboratory, sprung as a surprise to Swann, he appeared to perturb the operation of the magnetometer, located in a vault below the floor of the building and shielded by mu-metal shielding, an aluminum container, copper shielding and a superconducting shield. As if to add insult to injury, he then went on to "remote view" the interior of the apparatus, rendering by drawing a reasonable facsimile of its rather complex (and heretofore unpublished) construction. It was this latter feat that impressed me perhaps even more than the former, as it also eventually did representatives of the intelligence community. I wrote up these observations and circulated it among my scientific colleagues in draft form of what was eventually published as part of a conference proceeding [4].

In a few short weeks a pair of visitors showed up at SRI with the above report in hand. Their credentials showed them to be from the CIA. They knew of my previous background as a Naval Intelligence Officer and then civilian employee at the National Security Agency (NSA) several years earlier, and felt they could discuss their concerns with me openly. There was, they told me, increasing concern in the intelligence community about the level of effort in Soviet parapsychology being funded by the Soviet security services [5]; by Western scientific standards the field was considered nonsense by most working scientists. As a result they had been on the lookout for a research laboratory outside of academia that could handle a quiet, low-profile classified investigation, and SRI appeared to fit the bill. They asked if I could arrange an opportunity for them to carry out some simple experiments with Swann, and, if the tests proved satisfactory, would I consider a pilot program along these lines? I agreed to consider this, and arranged for the requested tests. [2]

The tests were simple, the visitors simply hiding objects in a box and asking Swann to attempt to describe the contents. The results generated in these experiments are perhaps captured most eloquently by the following example. In one test Swann said "I see something small, brown and irregular, sort of like a leaf or something that resembles it, except that it seems very much alive, like it's even moving!" The target chosen by one of the visitors turned out to be a small live moth, which indeed did look like a leaf. Although not all responses were quite so precise, nonetheless the integrated results were sufficiently impressive that in short order an eight-month, $49,909 Biofield Measurements Program was negotiated as a pilot study, a laser colleague Russell Targ who had had a long-time interest and involvement in parapsychology joined the program, and the experimental effort was begun in earnest.

Early Remote Viewing Results

During the eight-month pilot study of remote viewing the effort gradually evolved from the remote viewing of symbols and objects in envelopes and boxes, to the remote viewing of local target sites in the San Francisco Bay area, demarked by outbound experimenters sent to the site under strict protocols devised to prevent artifactual results. Later judging of the results were similarly handled by double-blind protocols designed to foil artifactual matching. Since these results have been presented in detail elsewhere, both in the scientific literature [6-8] and in popular book format [9], I direct the interested reader to these sources. To summarize, over the years the back-and-forth criticism of

Beginnings

protocols, refinement of methods, and successful replication of this type of remote viewing in independent laboratories [10-14], has yielded considerable scientific evidence for the reality of the phenomenon. Adding to the strength of these results was the discovery that a growing number of individuals could be found to demonstrate high-quality remote viewing, often to their own surprise, such as the talented Hella Hammid. As a separate issue, however, most convincing to our early program monitors were the results now to be described, generated under their own control.

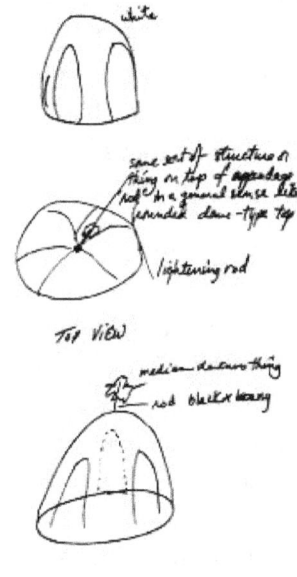
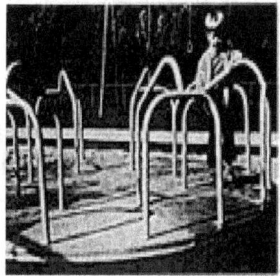

Figure 1 – Sketch of target by VI

Figure 2 - Target (merry-go-round)

First, during the collection of data for a formal remote viewing series targeting indoor laboratory apparatus and outdoor locations (a series eventually published in toto in the Proc. IEEE [7]), the CIA contract monitors, ever watchful for possible chicanery, participated as remote viewers themselves in order to critique the protocols. In this role three separate viewers, designated visitors V1 - V3 in the IEEE paper, contributed seven of the 55 viewings, several of striking quality. Reference to the IEEE paper for a comparison of descriptions/ drawings to pictures of the associated targets, generated by the contract monitors in their own viewings, leaves little doubt as to why the contract monitors came to the conclusion that there was something to remote viewing (see, for example, Figure 1 herein).

As summarized in the Executive Summary of the now-released Final Report [2] of the second year of the program, "The development of this capability at SRI has evolved to the point where visiting CIA personnel with no previous exposure to such concepts have performed well under controlled laboratory conditions (that is, generated target descriptions of sufficiently high quality to permit blind matching of descriptions to targets by independent judges)." What happened next, however, made even these results pale in comparison.

Coordinate Remote Viewing

To determine whether it was necessary to have a "beacon" individual at the target site, Swann suggested carrying out an experiment to remote view the planet Jupiter before the upcoming NASA Pioneer 10 fly by. In that case, much to his chagrin (and ours) he found a ring around Jupiter, and wondered if perhaps he had remote viewed Saturn by mistake. Our colleagues in astronomy were quite unimpressed as well, until the flyby revealed that an unanticipated ring did in fact exist. [3] Expanding the protocols yet further, Swann proposed a series of experiments in which the target was designated not by sending a "beacon" person to the target site, but rather by the use of geographical coordinates, latitude and longitude in degrees, minutes and seconds. Needless to say, this proposal seemed even more outrageous than "ordinary" remote viewing. The difficulties in taking this proposal seriously, designing protocols to eliminate the possibility of a combination of globe memorization and eidetic or

Beginnings

photographic memory, and so forth, are discussed in considerable detail in Reference [9]. Suffice it to say that investigation of this approach, which we designated Scanate (scanning by coordinate), eventually provided us with sufficient evidence to bring it up to the contract monitors and suggest a test under their control. A description of that test and its results, carried out in mid-1973 during the initial pilot study, are best presented by quoting directly from the Executive Summary of the Final Report of the second year's follow-up program [2]. The remote viewers were Ingo Swann and Pat Price, and the entire transcripts are available in the released documents [2].

In order to subject the remote viewing phenomena to a rigorous long distance test under external control, a request for geographical coordinates of a site unknown to subject and experimenters was forwarded to the OSI group responsible for threat analysis in this area. In response, SRI personnel received a set of geographical coordinates (latitude and longitude in degrees, minutes, and seconds) of a facility, hereafter referred to as the West Virginia Site. The experimenters then carried out a remote viewing experiment on a double-blind basis, that is, blind to experimenters as well as subject. The experiment had as its goal the determination of the utility of remote viewing under conditions approximating an operational scenario. Two subjects targeted on the site, a sensitive installation. One subject drew a detailed map of the building and grounds layout, the other provided information about the interior including code words, data subsequently verified by sponsor sources (report available from COTR).[4]

Since details concerning the site's mission in general, [5] and evaluation of the remote viewing test in particular, remain highly classified to this day, all that can be said is that interest in the client community was heightened considerably following this exercise.

Because Price found the above exercise so interesting, as a personal challenge he went on to scan the other side of the globe for a Communist Bloc equivalent and found one located in the Urals, the detailed description of which is also included in Ref. [2]. As with the West Virginia Site, the report for the Urals Site was also verified by personnel in the sponsor organization as being substantially correct.

What makes the West Virginia/Urals Sites viewings so remarkable is that these are not best-ever examples culled out of a longer list; these are literally the first two site-viewings carried out in a simulated operational-type scenario. In fact, for Price these were the very first two remote viewings in our program altogether, and he was invited to participate in yet further experimentation.

Operational Remote Viewing (Semipalatinsk, USSR)

Midway through the second year of the program (July 1974) our CIA sponsor decided to challenge us to provide data on a Soviet site of ongoing operational significance. Pat Price was the remote viewer. A description of the remote viewing, taken from our declassified final report [2], reads as given below. I cite this level of detail to indicate the thought that goes into such an "experiment" to minimize cueing while at the same time being responsive to the requirements of an operational situation. Again, this is not a "best-ever" example from a series of such viewings, but rather the very first operational Soviet target concerning which we were officially tasked. "To determine the utility of remote viewing under operational conditions, a long-distance remote viewing experiment was carried out on a sponsor designated target of current interest, an unidentified research center at Semipalatinsk, USSR.

This experiment, carried out in three phases, was under direct control of the COTR. To begin the experiment, the COTR furnished map coordinates in degrees, minutes and seconds. The only additional information provided was the designation of the target as an R&D test facility. The experimenters then closeted

Beginnings

themselves with Subject S1, gave him the map coordinates and indicated the designation of the target as an R&D test facility. A remote-viewing experiment was then carried out. This activity constituted Phase I of the experiment.

Figure 3 shows the subject's graphic effort for building layout; Figure 4 shows the subject's particular attention to a multistory gantry crane he observed at the site. Both results were obtained by the experimenters on a double-blind basis before exposure to any additional COTR-held information, thus eliminating the possibility of cueing. These results were turned over to the client representatives for evaluation. For comparison, an artist's rendering of the site as known to the COTR (but not to the experimenters until later) is shown in Figure 5.

Were the results not promising, the experiment would have stopped at this point. Description of the multistory crane, however, a relatively unusual target item, was taken as indicative of possible target acquisition. Therefore, Phase II was begun, defined by the subject being made "witting" (of the client) by client representatives who introduced themselves to the subject at that point; Phase II also included a second round of experimentation on the Semipalatinsk site with direct participation of client representatives in which further data were obtained and evaluated. As preparation for this phase, client representatives purposely kept themselves blind to all but general knowledge of the target site to minimize the possibility of cueing. The Phase II effort was focused on the generation of physical data that could be independently verified by other client sources, thus providing a calibration of the process.

The end of Phase II gradually evolved into the first part of Phase III, the generation of unverifiable data concerning the Semipalatinsk site not available to the client, but of operational interest nonetheless. Several hours of tape transcript and a notebook of drawings were generated over a two-week period.

The data describing the Semipalatinsk site were evaluated by the sponsor, and are contained in a separate report. In general,

Evidential Details

several details concerning the salient technology of the Semipalatinsk site appeared to dovetail with data from other sources, and a number of specific large structural elements were correctly described. The results contained noise along with the signal, but were nonetheless clearly differentiated from the chance results that were generated by control subjects in comparison experiments carried out by the COTR."

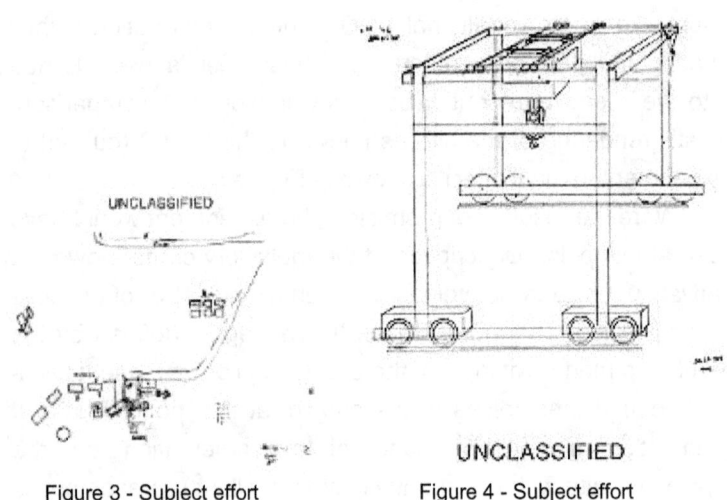

Figure 3 - Subject effort at building layout

Figure 4 - Subject effort construction crane

For discussion of the ambiance and personal factors involved in carrying out this experiment, along with further detail generated as Price (see Figure 6) "roamed" the facility, including detailed comparison of Price's RV-generated information with later determined "ground-truth reality," see the accompanying article by Russell Targ in the Journal of Scientific Exploration <http:// www.jse.com/>, Vol. 10, No. 1.

Additional experiments having implications for intelligence concerns were carried out, such as the remote viewing of cipher machine type apparatus, and the RV-sorting of sealed envelopes to differentiate those that contained letters with secret writing from those that did not. To discuss these here in detail would take us too far afield, but the interested reader can follow up by referring to the now-declassified project documents [2].

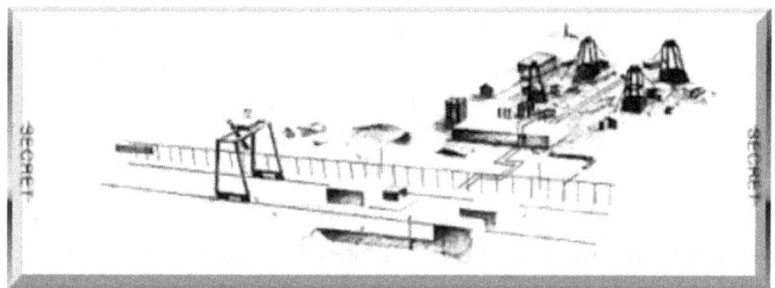

Figure 5 - Actual COTR rendering of Semipalatinsk, USSR target site.

Follow-on Programs

The above discussion brings us up to the end of 1975. As a result of the material being generated by both SRI and CIA remote viewers, interest in the program in government circles, especially within the intelligence community, intensified considerably and led to an ever increasing briefing schedule. This in turn led to an ever-increasing number of clients, contracts and tasking, and therefore expansion of the program to a multi-client base, and eventually to an integrated joint-services program under single-agency (DIA)[6] leadership. To meet the demand for the increased level of effort we first increased our professional staff by inviting Ed May to join the program in 1976, then screened and added to the program a cadre of remote viewers as consultants, and let subcontracts to increase our scope of activity.

As the program expanded, in only a very few cases could the client's identities and program tasking be revealed. Examples include a NASA-funded study negotiated early in the program by Russ Targ to determine whether the internal state of an electronic random-number-generator could be detected by RV processes [16], and a study funded by the Naval Electronics Systems Command to determine whether attempted remote viewing of

Evidential Details

distant light flashes would induce correlated changes in the viewer's brainwave (EEG) production [17]. For essentially all other projects, during my 14-yr. tenure at SRI, however, the identity of the clients and most of the tasking were classified and remain so today. (The exception was the occasional privately funded study.) We are told, however, that further declassification and release of much of this material is almost certain to occur.

What can be said, then, about further development of the program in the two decades following 1975?[7] In broad terms it can be said that much of the SRI effort was directed not so much toward developing an operational U.S. capability, but rather toward assessing the threat potential of its use against the U.S. by others.

The words 'threat assessment' were often used to describe the program's purpose during its development, especially during the early years. As a result much of the remote-viewing activity was carried out under conditions where ground-truth reality was a priori known or could be determined, such as the description of U.S. facilities and technological developments, the timing of rocket test firings and underground nuclear tests, and the location of individuals and mobile units. And, of course, we were responsive to requests to provide assistance during such events as the loss of an airplane or the taking of hostages, relying on the talents of an increasing cadre of remote-viewer/ consultants, some well-known in the field such as Keith Harary, and many who have not surfaced publicly until recently, such as Joe McMoneagle.

One might ask whether in this program RV-generated information was ever of sufficient significance as to influence decisions at a policy level. This is of course impossible to determine unless policymakers were to come forward with a statement in the affirmative. One example of a possible candidate is a study we performed at SRI during the Carter administration debates concerning proposed deployment of the mobile MX missile system.

In that scenario missiles were to be randomly shuffled from

Beginnings

Figure 6 - Left to right: Christopher Green,[2] Pat Price,[3] and Hal Puthoff. Picture taken following a successful experiment involving glider-ground RV.

silo to silo in a silo field, in a form of high-tech shell game. In a computer simulation of a twenty-silo field with randomly-assigned (hidden) missile locations, we were able, using RV-generated data, to show rather forcefully that the application of a sophisticated statistical averaging technique (sequential sampling) could in principle permit an adversary to defeat the system. I briefed these results to the appropriate offices at their request, and a written report with the technical details was widely circulated among groups responsible for threat analysis [18], and with some impact. What role, if any, our small contribution played in the mix of factors

---

[2] Dr. Christopher Green MD. Neurophysiology, received the CIA's National Intelligence Medal as a Scientific Advisory Board Member to the CIA's Directorate of Intelligence.

[3] One of the finest remote viewers ever, Pat Price, a former police commissioner and councilman in Burbank, CA, came to the Government's attention when he viewed officers, interiors, and files at the virtually unknown, nuclear hardened Naval Satellite Intelligence site in West Virginia. When the Pentagon was shown the data, Price was interrogated by the U.S. Defense Investigative Service who demanded to know who had breached security and how they did it. He is reputed to be the only viewer that could read numbers and letters on a target. Later he viewed inside the Soviet installation at Mount Narodnaya in the Ural Mountains. He went on to work for the CIA and is reputed to have died of a heart attack in July of 1975, in Las Vegas. Even though he was supposedly dead on arrival at the hospital, no autopsy was performed. Suspicions have always existed about the truth of his death. [author]

behind the enormously complex decision to cancel the program will probably never be known, and must of course a priori be considered in all likelihood negligible. Nonetheless, this is a prototypical example of the kind of tasking that by its nature potentially had policy implications.

Even though the details of the broad range of experiments, some brilliant successes, many total failures, have not yet been released, we have nonetheless been able to publish summaries of what was learned in these studies about the overall characteristics of remote viewing, as in Table 5 of Reference [8]. Furthermore, over the years we were able to address certain questions of scientific interest in a rigorous way and to publish the results in the open literature. Examples include the apparent lack of attenuation of remote viewing due to seawater shielding (submersible experiments) [8], the amplification of RV performance by use of error-correcting coding techniques [19, 20], and the utility of a technique we call associational remote viewing (ARV) to generate useful predictive information [21].8

As a sociological aside, we note that the overall efficacy of remote viewing in a program like this was not just a scientific issue. For example, when the Semipalatinsk data described earlier was forwarded for analysis, one group declined to get involved because the whole concept was unscientific nonsense, while a second group declined because, even though it might be real, it was possibly demonic; a third group had to be found. And, as in the case of public debate about such phenomena, the program's image was on occasion as likely to be damaged by an over enthusiastic supporter, as by a detractor. Personalities, politics and personal biases were always factors to be dealt with.

Official Statements/Perspectives

With regard to admission by the government of its use of remote viewers under operational conditions, officials have on occasion been relatively forthcoming. President Carter, in a speech to

Beginnings

college students in Atlanta in September 1995, is quoted by Reuters as saying that during his administration a plane went down in Zaire, and a meticulous sweep of the African terrain by American spy satellites failed to locate any sign of the wreckage. It was then "without my knowledge" that the head of the CIA (Adm. Stansfield Turner) turned to a woman reputed to have psychic powers. As told by Carter, "she gave some latitude and longitude figures. We focused our satellite cameras on that point and the plane was there." Independently, Turner himself also has admitted the Agency's use of a remote viewer (in this case, Pat Price).[9] And recently, in a segment taped for the British television series Equinox [22], Maj. Gen. Ed Thompson, Assistant Chief of Staff for Intelligence, U.S. Army (1977-1981), volunteered "I had one or more briefings by SRI and was impressed.... The decision I made was to set up a small, in-house, low-cost effort in remote viewing...."

Finally, a recent unclassified report [23] prepared for the CIA by the American Institutes for Research (AIR), concerning a remote viewing effort carried out under a DIA program called Star Gate (discussed in detail elsewhere in this volume), cites the roles of the CIA and DIA in the history of the program, including acknowledgment that a cadre of full-time government employees used remote viewing techniques to respond to tasking from operational military organizations. [10]

As information concerning the various programs spawned by intelligence-community interest is released, and the dialog concerning their scientific and social significance is joined, the results are certain to be hotly debated. Bearing witness to this fact are the companion articles in this volume by Ed May, Director of the SRI and SAIC programs since 1985, and by Jessica Utts and Ray Hyman, consultants on the AIR evaluation cited above. These articles address in part the AIR study. That study, limited in scope to a small fragment of the overall program effort, resulted in a conclusion that although laboratory research showed statistically

Evidential Details

significant results, use of remote viewing in intelligence gathering was not warranted.

Regardless of one's a priori position, however, an unimpassioned observer cannot help but attest to the following fact. Despite the ambiguities inherent in the type of exploration covered in these programs, the integrated results appear to provide unequivocal evidence of a human capacity to access events remote in space and time, however falteringly, by some cognitive process not yet understood. My years of involvement as a research manager in these programs have left me with the conviction that this fact must be taken into account in any attempt to develop an unbiased picture of the structure of reality.

Footnotes

1 - One example being the release of documents that are the subject of this report - see the memoir by Russell Targ.

2 - Since the reputation of the intelligence services is mixed among members of the general populace, I have on occasion been challenged as to why I would agree to cooperate with the CIA or other elements of the intelligence community in this work. My answer is simply that as a result of my own previous exposure to this community I became persuaded that war can almost always be traced to a failure in intelligence, and that therefore the strongest weapon for peace is good intelligence.

3 - This result was published by us in advance of the ring's discovery [9].

4 - Editor's footnote added here: COTR - Contracting Officer's Technical Representative.

5 - An NSA listening post at the Navy's Sugar Grove facility, according to intelligence-community chronicler Bamford [15]

6 - DIA - Defense Intelligence Agency. The CIA dropped out as a major player in the mid-seventies due to pressure on the Agency (unrelated to the RV Program) from the Church-Pike Congressional Committee.

7 - See also the contribution by Ed May elsewhere in this volume concerning his experiences from 1985 on during his tenure as Director.

8 - For example, one application of this technique yielded not only a published, statistically significant result, but also a return of $26,000 in 30 days in the silver futures market [21].

9 - The direct quote is given in Targ's contribution elsewhere in this volume.

10 - "From 1986 to the first quarter of FY 1995, the DoD paranormal psychology program received more than 200 tasks from operational military organizations requesting that the program staff apply a paranormal psychological technique know (sic) as "remote viewing" (RV) to attain information unavailable from other sources." [23]

References

[1] "*CIA Statement on 'Remote Viewing,*" CIA Public Affairs Office, 6 September 1995.

[2] Harold E. Puthoff and Russell Targ, "*Perceptual Augmentation Techniques,*" SRI Progress Report No. 3 (31 Oct. 1974) and Final Report (1 Dec. 1975) to the CIA, covering the period January 1974 through February 1975, the second year of the program. This effort was funded at the level of $149,555.

[3] H. E. Puthoff, "*Toward a Quantum Theory of Life Process,*" unpubl proposal, Stanford Research Institute (1972).

[4] H. E. Puthoff and R. Targ, "*Physics, Entropy and Psycho-kinesis,*" in Proc. Conf. Quantum Physics and Parapsychology (Geneva, Switzerland); (New York: Parapsychology Foundation, 1975).

[5] Documented in "*Paraphysics R&D - Warsaw Pact (U),*" DST-1810S-202-78, Defense Intelligence Agency (30 March 1978).

[6] R. Targ and H. E. Puthoff, "*Information Transfer under Conditions of Sensory Shielding,*" Nature 252, 602 (1974).

[7] H. E. Puthoff and R. Targ, "*A Perceptual Channel for Information*

Evidential Details

Transfer over Kilometer Distances: Historical Perspective and Recent Research," Proc. IEEE 64, 329 (1976).

[8] H. E. Puthoff, R. Targ and E. C. May, "*Experimental Psi Research: Implications for Physics,*" in *The Role of Consciousness in the Physical World*", edited by R. G. Jahn (AAAS Selected Symposium 57, Westview Press, Boulder, 1981).

[9] R. Targ and H. E. Puthoff, *Mind Reach* (Delacorte Press, New York, 1977).

[10] J. P. Bisaha and B. J. Dunne, "*Multiple Subject and Long-Distance Precognitive Remote Viewing of Geographical Locations,*" in Mind at Large, edited by C. T. Tart, H. E. Puthoff and R. Targ (Praeger, New York, 1979), p. 107.

[11] B. J. Dunne and J. P. Bisaha, "*Precognitive Remote Viewing in the Chicago Area: a Replication of the Stanford Experiment,*" J. Parapsychology 43, 17 (1979).

[12] R. G. Jahn, "*The Persistent Paradox of Psychic Phenomena: An Engineering Perspective,*" Proc. IEEE 70, 136 (1982).

[13] R. G. Jahn and B. J. Dunne, "*On the Quantum Mechanics of Consciousness with Application to Anomalous Phenomena,*" Found. Phys. 16, 721 (1986).

[14] R. G. Jahn and B. J. Dunne, *Margins of Reality* (Harcourt, Brace and Jovanovich, New York, 1987).

[15] J. Bamford, *The Puzzle Palace* (Penguin Books, New York, 1983) pp. 218-222.

[16] R. Targ, P. Cole and H. E. Puthoff, "*Techniques to Enhance Man/ Machine Communication,*" Stanford Research Institute Final Report on NASA Project NAS7-100 (August 1974).

[17] R. Targ, E. C. May, H. E. Puthoff, D. Galin and R. Ornstein, "*Sensing of Remote EM Sources* (Physiological Correlates)," SRI Intern'l Final Report on Naval Electronics Systems Command Project N00039-76-C-0077, covering the period November 1975 - to October 1976 (April 1978).

[18] H. E. Puthoff, "*Feasibility Study on the Vulnerability of the MPS System to RV Detection Techniques,*" SRI Internal Report, 15 April 1979; revised 2 May 1979.

[19] H. E. Puthoff, "*Calculator-Assisted Psi Amplification,*" Research in

Beginnings

Parapsychology 1984, edited by Rhea White and J. Solfvin (Scarecrow Press, Metuchen, NJ, 1985), p. 48.

[20] H. E. Puthoff, "*Calculator-Assisted Psi Amplification II: Use of the Sequential-Sampling Technique as a Variable-Length Majority-Vote Code,*" Research in Parapsychology 1985, edited by D. Weiner and D. Radin (Scarecrow Press, Metuchen, NJ, 1986), p. 73.

[21] H. E. Puthoff, "*ARV (Associational Remote Viewing) Applications,*" Research in Parapsychology 1984, edited by Rhea White and J. Solfvin (Scarecrow Press, Metuchen, NJ, 1985), p. 121.

[22] "*The Real X-Files*", Independent Channel 4, England (shown 27 August 1995); to be shown in the U.S. on the Discovery Channel.

[23] M. D. Mumford, A. M. Rose and D. Goslin, "*An Evaluation of Remote Viewing: Research and Applications*", American Institutes for Research (September 29, 1995).

Copyright 1996 by Dr. H.E. Puthoff.
Permission to redistribute granted, but only in complete and unaltered form.

[The footnotes are designed to facilitate a greater understanding of Remote Viewing pioneers, but are not original. None of Dr. Puthoff's text was altered.]

THE 1973 REMOTE VIEWING PROBE OF THE PLANET JUPITER'S DISCOVERED RING
as viewed by military RV instructor Ingo Swann

(The Planet Jupiter ring discovery remote viewing) *Experiment #46 lay obscure between 1974 and 1979. No continuing attempt was made to feedback other of its categories, and the SRI* (Stanford Research Institute) *work progressed along more immediately fruitful* (confirmational) *lines.*

(Six years later) *The 1979* (Voyager 2) *scientific discovery and* (the July 9, 1979) *confirmation of the* (Jupiter's) *Jovian Ring came as one of the larger shocks - and surprises -- in astronomical history.*

Targeted Reading

Because of its capabilities, Remote Viewing disinformation exists which discourages further interest. This list was assembled to help people locate books directly from members of the program involved in this most fascinating component of United States Military History.

Books by Members of the U.S. Military Program

McMoneagle, Joseph W.

- *Mind Trek*; Hampton Roads, 1993
- *The Ultimate Time Machine*; Hampton Roads, 1998
- *Remote Viewing Secrets*; Hampton Roads, 2000
- *The Stargate Chronicles*; Hampton Roads, 2002
- *Memoirs of a Psychic Spy: The Remarkable Life of U. S. Government Remote Viewer 001*; Hampton Roads, 2006

Buchanan, Leonard

- *The Seventh Sense – The Secrets of Remote Viewing as Told by a "Psychic Spy" for the U.S. Military*; Paraview Pocket Books, 2003

- *Remote Viewing Methods - Remote Viewing and Remote Influencing*; DVD, 2004

Smith, Paul H.

- *Reading the Enemy's Mind - Inside Stargate - America's Psychic Espionage Program*; Tor non-fiction, 2005

Morehouse, David A.

- *Psychic Warrior – Inside the CIA's Stargate Program: The True Story of a Soldiers Espionage and Awakening*; St Martin's Press, 1996

Targeted Reading

- *Nonlethal Weapons: War Without Death*; Praeger Publishers, 1996

- *Remote Viewing: The Complete User's Manual for Coordinate Remote Viewing*; Sounds True Publishers, 2011

Atwater, F. Holmes

- *Captain of My Ship, Master of My Soul: Living with Guidance*; Hampton Roads Publishing, 2001

Puthoff, Harold E. with Russell Targ

- *Mind Reach - Scientists Look at Psychic Abilities*; Delacorte, 1977 & New World Library, 2004

Swann, Ingo

- *To Kiss the Earth Goodbye*; Hawthorne, New York, 1975
- *Star Fire*, Dell non-fiction, 1978
- *Natural ESP: The ESP Core and its Raw Characteristics* with Harold E. Puthoff; Bantam Books, 1987
- *Everybody's Guide to Natural ESP: Unlocking The Extrasensory Power of Your Mind*; Jeremy P. Tharcher Imprint, 1991
- *Your Nostradamus Factor*; Fireside Press, 1993
- *Remote Viewing & ESP From The Inside Out*; DVD

Targ, Russell

- *Mind Race: Understanding and Using Psychic Abilities*, with Keith Harary; Ballantine Books, 1984
- *Miracles of Mind: Exploring Nonlocal Consciousness and Spiritual Healing*; New World Library, 1999
- *Limitless Mind: A Guide to Remote Viewing and Transformation of Consciousness*; New World Library, 2004
- *Do you See What I See?*; ESP and the C.I.A. and the Meaning of Life; Hampton Roads, 2010
- *The Reality of ESP: A Physicists Proof of Psychic Abilities*; Quest Books, 2012

Evidential Details

Other Sources

<u>Monroe, Robert</u>

- *Journeys Out of the Body*; Three Rivers Press, 1992
- *Ultimate Journey*; Three Rivers Press, 1996

<u>Radin, Dean I.</u>

- *The Conscious Universe: The Scientific Truth of Psychic Phenomena*; Harper Edge, 1997

- *Entangled Minds: Extrasensory Experiences in a Quantum Reality*, Paraview Pocket Books, 2006

- Moreno, Jonathon D. - *Mind Wars: Brain Science and the Military in the 21st Century*; Bellevue Literary Press, 2012

- Schnabel, Jim – *Remote Viewers: The Secret History of America's Psychic Spies*; Dell–non-fiction, 1997

- McRae, Ronald – *Mind Wars: The true story of Government Research into the Military Potential of Psychic Weapons*; St Martin's Press, 1984

- Gruber, Elmar – *Psychic Wars – Parapsychology in Espionage – and Beyond*; Blandford, London, 1999

- Dong, Paul with Thomas Rafill – *China's Super Psychics*; Marlowe & Co., New York, 1997

- Brown, Courtney - *Remote Viewing: The Science and Theory of Nonphysical Perception*; Farsight Press, United Kingdom, 2005

- Foerstel, Herbert – *Federal Control of American Science and Technology*; Praeger, 1993

- Ostrander, Sheila and Lynn Schroeder – *Psychic Discoveries Behind the Iron Curtain*; Prentice Hall, 1970

Evidential Details

Additional Taskings

Lae City Airport, New Guinea - July, 1937 – Peer into the cockpit for the last flight of the vanished pilot **Amelia Earhart**. Learn of the plane's unknown final flight trajectory, cockpit circumstances and final thoughts in her last minute of life. Entered into Purdue University's Earhart Special Collection Library, the book includes a "how to find the debris field" location map with yardages and points of reference including our military report's flight scenario. With the continuous failure of other groups, insiders have blogged that our scenario is the one worth pursuing. Opposed by some businesses as the book that end the mystery.

Ötzal Alps Mountains - Italian-Austrian border ~ 3,300 BC – Follow the trail of Europe's archeological "show of the century". Learn the whereabouts of **Ötzi the Iceman**'s unknown home camp and why and how he died alone in the mountains which some still regard as a Neolithic crime scene. This book includes remote viewing maps, pre-death tool drawings, including an undiscovered tool, his cabin, and the world's only real time portrait considered significant enough that the Museum in Bolzano, Italy obtained its copywrite release for Ötzi's 20th Anniversary exhibit. Interwoven with scientific quotation, this account also includes specifics of his tribal life in what we identified first as the Langtaufers Valley. The book provides Ötzi's previously unknown eight day course through the mountains sighting modern Alpine trail numbers. Learn the cause for his violent death which is the only solution that unifies the various theories.

The Civil War's Biggest Mystery, State of Maryland - September, 1862 – Considered an unsolvable whodunit, this little known, but most significant mystery in America's Civil War resolves who lost Confederate **General Robert E. Lee's** top secret **Special Order 191**. The result was the battles of South Mountain and Harper's Ferry, leading directly to the bloodiest day in American History at Antietam Creek. The upshot was the timing of

Additional Taskings

the Emancipation Proclamation..With information from the National Park Service, the book provides aerial campground maps and reveals the previously unknown who, why, when, where and how these orders found their way into the Union General's hands. This book also provides the world's first clinical determination on Union Commander George McClellan's psychological problems.

Last Stand Hill - Little Big Horn River - Montana - June, 1876 – This is History's only documentation of **General George Armstrong Custer**'s last stand from the viewpoints of the victors and the vanquished. Read about Chief Sitting Bull's and Custer's battle thoughts. Learn of his true cause of Custer's death and the amazing reasons his body is likely not in his tomb at West Point. You get new, remote viewing generated, battle maps with a drawing of Custer's last fighting stance, a near death facial close-up drawing and, since he was never photographed, the world's only full page color portrait of Indian War Chief *Crazy Horse*.

Execution Square - Rouen, France - May, 1431 – Go right to the burning scaffold in the market square for the burning of the military heroine lost in the mists of time - **Joan of Arc**. Highlighted are her military successes, capture, and some trial excerpts. These sessions provide an amazingly detailed architectural description of Rouen's medieval square exactly as Joan saw it. Learn of the perpetrator's underlying motivations and the fear of the medieval spectators as well as the British soldiers. McMoneagle's renowned artwork includes what the scene really looked like when she was chained down and includes History's only portrait of this previously faceless heroine.

www.ingramcontent.com/pod-product-compliance
Lightning Source LLC
Chambersburg PA
CBHW050639300426
44112CB00012B/1857